Women and Millenarian Protest in Meiji Japan

Women and Millenarian Protest in Meiji Japan

Deguchi Nao and Ōmotokyō

Emily Groszos Ooms

East Asia Program
Cornell University
Ithaca, New York 14853

The *Cornell East Asia Series* publishes manuscripts on a wide variety of scholarly topics pertaining to East Asia. Manuscripts are published on the basis of camera-ready copy provided by the volume author or editor.

Inquiries should be addressed to Editorial Board, Cornell East Asia Series, East Asia Program, Cornell University, 140 Uris Hall, Ithaca, New York 14853.

ISSN 1050-2955
ISBN 0-939657-61-9

For Herman
  and our children, Renata and Jonathan

Contents

Foreword

The role of women in Japan's new religions has been a crucial one. Nakayama Miki (1798-1887) founded Tenrikyō, Kitamura Sayo (1900-1967) founded Tenshō Kōtai Jingūkyō, and Kotani Kimi (1901-1971) co-founded Reiyūkai Kyōdan. Here, Emily Ooms expands and refines our understanding of women's roles in the creation of new modes of religious thought and action in her insightful analysis of the life and teachings of Deguchi Nao (1837-1918) and the religion she founded, Ōmotokyō. By placing Nao within a broad historical context that includes socioeconomic, political, and cultural factors, Ooms also shows how women's experience and consciousness of rapid change in late nineteenth century Japan inspired new forms of resistance and protest.

Typically, studies of the Meiji period (1868-1912) have emphasized the relative ease with which Japan developed a modern industry, bureaucracy, and military, focusing on the political and entrepreneurial elite responsible for this "progress" and ignoring those upon whom it was imposed, particularly women. Recent scholarship, however, has challenged the notion that women played a "marginal" role in Japanese history, documenting their many contributions and introducing gender as a necessary category of analysis. Even in industry, it was women workers who produced Japan's major exports down to the end of World War I, and they performed not simply as passive pawns of their parents and the state but acted for their own positive goals of autonomy and increased income as well. Mikiso Hane has demonstrated that modernization came at a tremendous social cost paid by the poor, the disadvantaged, and women. It is clear that any effort to understand Japanese history must now include the experiences of the "other half" of the population.

As Ooms discusses in her final chapter, one major consequence of Japan's development into a modern state was the further confinement of women to the private sphere. In Japan's early modern era (1600-1868), both peasant and merchant women worked in the family fields and businesses and occasionally participated in village assemblies. Although they most often did so as representatives of their households, a designation that transcended traditional gender roles, they were still quite active in the public sphere. Moreover, in both town and country, household employments for men and women provided monetary as well as non-monetary returns.

Samurai women, in contrast, could not perform the service demanded of their men, and therefore lacked any access to public visibility. In this respect, the model of appropriate female behavior put forward by Meiji statesmen was most probably drawn from memories of their mothers, samurai women who lived in relative seclusion and stressed the "womanly values" of modesty, submission, and silent forebearance in the face of hardship. The turmoil of the popular rights movement in the early 1880s only served to confirm this assumption that women should stay in the home and out of politics. Not surprisingly, the Civil Code of 1890 placed severe limitations on the ability of women to manage their own finances; without the endorsement of a man, a woman could no longer conduct business the way her mother had. Furthermore, modern bureaucratic institutions and industrial growth generated an increasing separation of work and residence. Once men began to receive a salary, the non-remunerated labor of women was rendered invisible.

Despite the exclusion of women from the public sphere and the concomitant redefinition of respectable women as "good wives and wise mothers," not all women accepted these limitations. In an age when most women were illiterate, Higuchi Ichiyō (1872-1896) mastered not only the standard vocabulary but classical Japanese as well. She spoke and wrote in her own voice, a voice she refused to allow to be labeled either feminine or masculine. Before she died at the age of 24, she had attracted the attention of Japan's most prestigious male novelists and, perhaps more difficult to achieve, the admiration of male students at Tokyo Imperial University as well. Like Deguchi Nao and the other female founders of new religions, she transcended the circumscribed role assigned to those of her sex through the power of her cognitive abilities.

Unfortunately, Higuchi Ichiyō was one of only a handful of women who achieved recognition or notoriety in Meiji Japan. The early 1880s was a period of possibilities in which many Japanese commoners, including women, hoped that they might have a say in the institutions that ruled their lives. They even took advantage of a new forum temporarily available to men and women alike -- the public speech. At political meetings and in public lectures, women like Kishida Toshiko (1863-1901) and Fukuda Hideko (1868-1927) encouraged women to organize discussion groups and public-speaking societies, to pursue their own education, and to strive for equality with men. Instead of the subordinate and apolitical roles for women promoted by government leaders, they proposed that women be allowed to manage their own resources and be treated as partners in the process of building Japan into a strong nation. They were optimistic, but their hopes were thwarted when the government enacted new public security regulations in 1890 which prohibited women from engaging in any political activities. Precisely because they were women, these political activists were subjected to harsher repression than were men.

By the turn of the century, government repression and the hardships suffered by the disadvantaged in the march of Japanese industrialization drove men and women political activists to become more extreme in their criticism of government policies. The most radical of the lot, Kanno Suga (1881-1911), expressed in revolutionary political terms what Deguchi Nao said in her religious messages. Both women completely rejected the capitalistic model of society pursued by the Meiji State and indeed denied the legitimacy of that state itself. The paths they sought would have led to a similar end -- the destruction of the imperial system and the creation of a decent life for the poor, the oppressed, and women. But while Kanno joined the anarchist movement and actively participated in an unsuccessful plot to assassinate the Meiji Emperor, Nao struggled to persuade people that a god, Ushitora-no-Konjin, would destroy the current evil world and establish a divine paradise in its place if only they would act in accordance with her teachings.

Western scholars have made considerable efforts to elucidate the parameters of anti-government criticism in prewar Japan and the discourse and practice of socialist and anarchist groups. This includes studies of nineteenth century social movements which gave voice to millennial aspirations, especially the expectation that the restoration of the emperor would sweep away the inequities of the Tokugawa state and usher in a new divine era. Nevertheless, since the peasants who called for world renewal and the elimination of the wealthy obviously had no chance of achieving their goals, little attention has been paid to the content of their thought and they have been relegated to the margins of history. However, considering how seldom even the most practical political revolutionaries are successful, we should not be so quick to condemn religious millenarian movements for their unrealistic aims. As Ooms argues, the articulation of a new vision of human community critical of the status quo can, in itself, constitute a significant form of political resistance.

In the case of Ōmotokyō, it was the woman founder, Deguchi Nao, not her male follower and organizer, Onisaburō (1871-1948), who articulated the most radical critique of existing society. As a political actor, but one who was forced by her sex to stand outside the political system, Nao took advantage of the traditional female role of medium for the gods to express a vision of reality that accorded with her own experience and expectations. Although she first saw herself as the passive instrument for Ushitora-no-Konjin and allowed Onisaburō to manipulate her message, it was through her "spirit possession" (*kamigakari*) that she gained the confidence to express her own assumptions about what the god wanted and to challenge Onisaburō's efforts to keep Ōmotokyō safely within the confines of government-approved religions. By the end of the Russo-Japanese War (1905), she was predicting not only the imminent demise of the Japanese state but the entire world as well.

Ooms' analysis of gender in the Japanese new religions raises broadly comparative questions that point the way to a deeper understanding of women's roles in history. Why in Japanese religions do we so often find that it is women rather than men who voice radical renunciations of existing society? With the exception of the Shakers and the Christian Scientists, most new religions founded in the nineteenth century -- the Taiping God worshippers in China, the Bahai faith in Iran, and the Mormons in the United States -- trace their origin to prophecies made by men. In Japan, however, women prophets were more successful in acquiring positions of authority and influence beyond their immediate households and in establishing new religious organizations based on their own visions of reality. Caught in the contradiction between a specific system of conventional morality which made their suffering a virtue and the pressure of socioeconomic change which no longer rewarded suffering, a few extraordinary women succeeded in articulating a different vision of human community in which their lives took on new value and meaning. How Deguchi Nao achieved this new meaning for herself and others is the subject of this book.

Anne Walthall
University of California, Irvine

Acknowledgements

When a manuscript takes as much time as this one has to see the light of published day, the list of people to be thanked is very long indeed. I would like to take this opportunity to formally acknowledge the many individuals whose support and expertise enabled me to complete this book. I shall begin with my teachers at the University of Chicago where I was a graduate student in the 1970s. Professors Bernard Cohn, Harry Harootunian, Tetsuo Najita and the late Joseph Kitagawa shared their knowledge of cultural theory and Japanese history with me and inspired me to think more creatively and critically about religion and politics.

I am also grateful to the many members of Ōmotokyō I met while in Japan in 1976-77 doing research for the master's thesis on which this book is based. In order to obtain additional information about Deguchi Nao and to observe the current rituals and festivals of the religion she founded, I often visited Ōmotokyō headquarters in Ayabe, Kameoka, and Tokyo. I was always welcomed warmly on these occasions. Everyone took an interest in my work and willingly answered all of my questions. In particular, Hino Iwao and Najima Hiroshi provided essential logistical and scholarly assistance. More recently, the staff of the Oomoto Foundation helped me to obtain the photographs which appear in this book. I am very grateful for their cooperation.

While writing my thesis, I often turned to friends and family for inspiration when my own enthusiasm for the project waned. For their unflagging support and infinite patience, I thank Regina Bowgierd, Sherry Engstrom, Miranda Ferrell, Elizabeth S. Groszos, Stephen J. Groszos, Catherine Garcia-Patterson, Elizabeth Harrison, Sonia Jacobson, Stephanie Kalfayan, John Kulczyski, Judith LeFevre, Kyoko Nakamura, Jessica Schneider, Cynthia Shambaugh, Ueda Yasunori, Ueda Shizuko, and Victoria Wike.

Although I had no intention of publishing my thesis when I completed it in 1984, several friends encouraged me to do so. Eventually, the manuscript was brought to the attention of Robert Smith, former editor of Cornell University's East Asia Series. I would like to thank Professor Smith and his successor, David McCann, for giving me this opportunity to share my work with others. I am particularly indebted to managing editor Karen Smith for guiding me so expertly and patiently through the complicated process of formatting the book.

In the course of revising the manuscript and preparing it for publication, a number of people provided invaluable support and assistance for which I am deeply grateful. Foremost is my friend and mentor Anne Walthall. Her enthusiasm for my work and her firm belief that it should be made available to others were a major source of inspiration. It was in large part her perseverance and support which enabled me to bring this project to fruition. In addition, I would like to thank Susan Mann for her careful reading of an early version of the manuscript; Cindy Nulty for facilitating the conversion of the original typewritten text into computerized form; Helen Hardacre and Sally Hastings for their suggestions about updating and expanding the bibliography; and Francesca Bray and Leslie Pincus for their advice and moral support.

In the final stages of manuscript preparation, I relied heavily on the expert help of three friends whose generous contributions of time and energy were crucial to the successful completion of this book. Emy Murakawa's steadfast commitment to getting the job done and getting it done right, along with her wonderful sense of humor, carried me through the tedious and often frustrating process of typesetting and formatting the text. I am very grateful for her tireless efforts on my behalf and for her companionship and support. Lynn Naliboff assisted me with the final editing and proofreading of the manuscript. Her thoughtful criticism and suggestions enabled me to clarify many points in the text. I am also grateful to James DeNardo for creating the map of the Ayabe region and the diagram of Nao's cosmology. His incisive comments on the latter resulted in substantial improvements to my original version.

My most profound gratitude is reserved for my husband, Herman Ooms, who sustained me emotionally and intellectually throughout this long endeavor. Without his encouragement and support, I could not have completed this project. It is to him and to our children, Renata and Jonathan, that I dedicate this book.

Introduction

Ōmotokyō is one of Japan's earliest "new religions" (*shinkō shūkyō*), the generic term for a large number and variety of lay associations which were organized independently of established religious institutions in the nineteenth and twentieth centuries. Syncretistic in doctrine and practice, the new religions contain Buddhist, Shinto, Christian, and folk religious elements. They are not, however, merely derivative of these traditional religions, for the men and women who founded them articulated new visions of reality and created new forms of group association and ritual practice. In the last two decades, much has been written in English about the new religions, but Ōmotokyō has received little more than cursory treatment.

Today, Ōmotokyō is a relatively small (although thriving) religious organization with an official membership of just under 165,000. The group maintains large worship and administrative facilities in Ayabe and Kameoka, and smaller branch offices in other cities. Lay priests minister to the needs of members through ancestral, celebratory, purification, and healing rites, group prayer and meditation. Each year, several major festivals are held in Ayabe which attract thousands of members from all over Japan. The group places a great emphasis on practicing and preserving the traditional Japanese arts, particularly the tea ceremony, aikido, *kendō*, *Nō* drama, ceramics, and calligraphy. Unlike a number of other new religions, Ōmotokyō is non-proselytizing and pursues its goal of world peace through active participation in international ecumenical movements. Since the mid-1940s, Ōmoto leaders have assiduously avoided any involvement in national political affairs. But culture did not always displace politics in Ōmotokyō doctrine and practice: for much of its early history, religion and politics were inseparable in Ōmotokyō and its relationship with the state was an antagonistic one.

1

In this book, I focus on the events leading up to Ōmotokyō's establishment in 1898 by Deguchi Nao (1837-1918) and Deguchi Onisaburō (1871-1948) and on the group's initial development into a radical millenarian cult in accordance with Nao's eschatological and utopian revelations.[1] The book provides an account of Nao's life and follows her activities through the close of the Russo-Japanese War in 1905, when her prophecies failed and Onisaburō lead the group in new directions. I intentionally circumscribed the scope of the study to allow for a more detailed examination of the social, economic, and cultural contexts of Nao's life and thought. I was particularly interested in exploring the political dimensions of Ōmotokyō's early history and the ways in which gender and class informed Nao's construction of a new vision of reality in conflict with the ideologies of the Meiji state.

This early phase of Ōmotokyō's history coincides with Japan's development into a modern nation-state and emergence as a military power in East Asia. Grounded in the experience and consciousness of a woman who lived in poverty for much of her life and who was unrelenting in her radical criticism of the Meiji state, the history of Ōmotokyō provides a unique perspective on the transformations in Japanese society and culture which occurred during the late nineteenth and early twentieth centuries. At the time I initiated this research, historians were just beginning to deconstruct the singular story of economic and social progress that adherents of modernization theory had claimed for the Meiji period (1868-1912). Not surprisingly, much of this new research has not focused on the male economic and political elite that engineered the Meiji "miracle," but on those at whose expense that miracle was achieved -- women, factory workers, the dispossessed peasantry, and the urban poor (e.g., Bernstein, 1980, 1991; Danly, 1981; Hane, 1982, 1988; Kidd, 1978; Sievers, 1983; and Tsurumi, 1990). This book is part of this ongoing effort to document the daily lives and thinking of those men and women who neither shared the Meiji state's vision of Japan's future nor benefitted from its policies and to identify the new forms of protest and resistance they created in response to state exploitation and oppression.

The convergence of religious belief and social protest, spiritual salvation and political emancipation, that one finds in the writings of Deguchi Nao is a common feature of millenarian movements both historically and cross-culturally. In Japan, the periodic occurrence of

---

[1] Japanese names are written in Japanese order, surname first.

popular belief in the imminent advent of the millennium has been well-documented by social historians and scholars of Japanese religion. However, it is generally acknowledged that Ōmotokyō, in the early years when Nao's influence was strongest (1900-1905), represents the most complete manifestation of millenarian thought and action in Japanese history. This is because Nao's millennial aspirations served a paradgmatic rather than supplemental function in the development of her religious doctrine and practice, providing the basic framework in terms of which she structured her new vision of reality and defined appropriate human behavior and action. Through multiple experiences of spirit possession or *kamigakari*, Nao came to see herself as the preeminent spokesperson for a powerful god who had decided to destroy the present evil world and establish in its place a divine utopia. In this respect, Nao's condemnation of Meiji society and its ruling elite is an essential component of her millenarian world view. Deeply concerned with the problem of human suffering and the abuse of power, she envisioned a new society in which virtuous human beings lived in peace and harmony with each other and the gods. Nao's orientation is thus both this-worldly and other-worldly, grounded in the present, yet focused on the future. The fact that she believed that radical social transformation could only be accomplished through divine intervention does not diminish the value of her social criticism or political resistance. Rather, it forces us to reconsider the linkages between religion, ideology, and politics, and to look more closely at those forms of social protest which are articulated in religious terms. The writings of Deguchi Nao provide us with a rare opportunity to understand the aspirations and concerns of a Meiji woman struggling to make sense of her own suffering and to resolve what she perceived as a major crisis in contemporary human affairs.

Nao's experience of *kamigakari* was a critical turning point in her life and the principal source of her religious authority and revelations. In fact, most founders of new religions, like Nao, began their careers as religious practitioners and organizers through a spontaneous experience of spirit possession which they later learned to control. Although this is generally recognized as a common characteristic of the new religions, little attention has been given to how this has affected their doctrine and practice. Before proceeding with an analysis of Nao's thought, I found it necessary to re-examine the phenomenon of spirit possession, particularly its creative and liberating dimensions. Accordingly, this book takes as its point of departure a discussion of Deguchi Nao's first experience of *kamigakari*.

Map 1. *Ayabe and the surrounding region.*

I
Kamigakari: A Source
of Transformative Knowledge

The term *kamigakari* means, literally, the possession (*kakaru* or *tsuku*) of the human body by a spiritual being (*kami*).[2] *Kami*, however, are not the only kind of possessing spirits or *tsukimono*: the spirits of animals (especially foxes and badgers), nature spirits, ancestral spirits, the souls of the dead, wandering ghosts, or even Buddhas (*hotoke*) may also possess people. In the state of trance which characterizes *kamigakari*, the possessed individual speaks and can respond to questions. It is believed, however, that these words are not his or her own conscious utterances, but the words of the *tsukimono* (Sakurai, 1974:195).

Kamigakari has been a common feature of Japanese folk religion since ancient times and references to it can be found in the *Kojiki* and the *Nihonshoki* (Sakurai, 1974:69). Professional mediums, shamans, ascetics, and even Buddhist and Shinto priests who could control such states of trance played important roles in village life as curers, exorcists, diviners, and primary participants in community rituals. The religious practitioners best known for their use of *kamigakari* include the blind *itako* and the Shinto *miko*, both of whom are female mediums, as well as the *yamabushi* or male shamans associated with various mountain cults. Instances of spontaneous *kamigakari* were also very common, especially as both physical and mental illnesses were often attributed to possession by malevolent spirits.

Deguchi Nao's first experience of *kamigakari* occurred when she was fifty-five years old. Shortly after the lunar new year, 1892, she suddenly found herself possessed by a spirit who claimed to be Ushitora-no-

---

[2]"*Kamigakari*," the colloquial word for spirit possession, is usually written in *hiragana*. The scholarly terms now used for spirit possession are *shinrei no hyōi* and *hyōrei*. *Hyōi* means either *yorisugaru* (to cling to, to rely on) or *nori-utsuru* (to possess, to inspire).

Konjin.[3] At that time Nao, impoverished and recently widowed, was struggling to support herself and her two youngest children by collecting and selling old rags and working part time in silk reeling factories. Since both occupations required Nao to walk great distances, she was often out until very late at night. When she finally returned home, she would gently awaken her daughters, Sumi and Ryō, and prepare dinner for them. But as Sumi, who was eleven years old at the time, has recorded in her memoirs, Nao's behavior was very different on that cold, snowy night in January, 1892. She stormed into the house, shouting in a loud but dignified voice which Sumi compared to that of a great general, and ordered her daughters to go pray at a shrine in the village. Sumi was so frightened by the angry tone in her mother's voice that she did not even take the time to put on her *geta*, but ran out the door barefooted, carrying her wooden sandals in her hands. When Sumi and Ryō returned home a short while later, they found their mother by the well in the backyard dousing herself with buckets of cold water (Yasumaru, 1977:74-75).

This was how Nao's first *kamigakari* began. It lasted for another thirteen days during which Nao fasted and performed frequent cold water ablutions. Nao's experience of spirit possession was characterized by very powerful physical sensations. She felt as though some living thing had entered her body and lodged itself in her lower abdomen. She felt heavier and stronger than she ever had before and the muscles in her back stiffened, forcing her to stand very erect with her chest thrust forward. The tension that filled her whole body made her tremble and when she sat down, her feet shook, making a thumping sound on the floor. Sometimes the *tsukimono* emitted only loud groans, but other times it spoke in a deep, harsh voice very different from Nao's own voice (Yasumaru, 1977:82-83). In fact, the two often conversed: Nao, in her normal voice, would question the spirit or reprimand him for his rudeness and the spirit would reply in

---

[3] According to the popular Shugendō tradition, Ushitora-no-Konjin was the hot-tempered guardian of the northeast direction who, at the slightest provocation, would put his curse of the "seven deaths" on someone. Kawate Bunjirō, the founder of Konkōkyō, was also possessed by Ushitora-no-Konjin. However, he claimed to reveal the god's true identity as the creator of the world and the savior of mankind (Hori, 1968:233-235). Several months prior to her *kamigakari*, Nao participated in an exorcism ceremony conducted by a Konkōkyō missionary at the home of one of her daughters (Yasumaru, 1977:79-80). Thus, she was aware of the conflicting interpretations of Ushitora-no-Konjin's identity. It was in part this knowledge that led her to doubt the validity of her own kamigakari -- if the spirit was the great god he claimed to be, why would he choose a poor, uneducated woman like Nao as the medium for his revelations? Chapter III contains a more detailed analysis of Ushitora-no-Konjin.

Deguchi Nao, ca. 1895

his usual loud, authoritarian manner. One of these dialogues, believed to be the first, is recorded as follows:

> Spirit: I am Ushitora-no-Konjin!
>
> Nao: Aren't you deceiving me with such words?
>
> Spirit: Because I am Ushitora-no-Konjin, I do not lie! If I should be wrong in what I say by even half the width of a hair, then there would be no gods in this world!
>
> Nao: Are you really such an important god? Don't foxes and badgers deceive people?
>
> Spirit: I am not a fox or a badger. I am the god who will reconstruct the three thousand worlds...
>
> Nao: Is what you say true?
>
> Spirit: If it were a lie, I would not go to all this trouble! (quoted in Yasumaru, 1977:83-84)

Nao, however, was not convinced. Deciding that she had been possessed by a clever and malicious fox,[4] she visited religious specialists in the hope of having it exorcised. These attempts at exorcism not only ended in failure but also induced even more violent bouts of *kamigakari* (Yasumaru, 1977:88-89). By the following year, Nao was still unable to either exorcise the spirit or control her states of possession. The acute physical symptoms of the *kamigakari* together with the ascetic regimen she adopted to reduce them made it impossible for her to lead a normal life. In addition, she had become a terrible nuisance in the community: the angry spirit threatened her neighbors, shouting insults at them and ordering them to leave their homes. The dialogues with the spirit also continued, becoming more and more elaborate (Yasumaru, 1977:90-91). In March, 1893, a series of fires broke out in Ayabe and the spirit declared that he had set them to punish the people for their evil ways. Nao's neighbors finally decided that she had gone insane. She was accused of arson and put in jail. Later, when someone else confessed to the crime, Nao was released from jail and confined to her home for forty days (Yasumaru, 1977:96-99).

---

[4] In her book *The Catalpa Bow* (1976:301), Carmen Blacker describes an incident of fox possession which seems quite similar to Nao's experience of *kamigakari*. It was originally recorded by a psychiatrist employed in a Tokyo hospital in the 1890s. Other examples of spirit possession can be found in her chapters on "The Ascetic's Power" and "Exorcism."

This period of enforced isolation marks the beginning of Nao's career as a religious practitioner, for she finally decided to believe the raging spirit which had possessed her. Fully accepting her new role as the *kami*'s mouthpiece in the present world, she vowed to abandon worldly concerns and devote her life to the realization of the *kami*'s will (Yasumaru, 1977:101). At the same time, the violent convulsions and shouting which had characterized her states of *kamigakari* ceased. Instead, she began to write down rather than utter the words of the spirit -- first with a nail on the soft plaster walls of her jail cell and later, at home, on rough scraps of paper (Yasumaru, 1977:103). Nao had never learned how to write so her sudden ability to do so was interpreted as a form of automatic writing -- a calm, trance-like state in which the medium records the thoughts of a controlling spirit. She would continue to do this almost every day for the rest of her life. The collection of these writings is called the *Ofudesaki* (*Tip of the Brush*).

This shift from an oral to a written mode of communication represents the successful culmination of Nao's efforts to control her wild states of *kamigakari*. The community acknowledged this change in Nao. She was no longer regarded as a crazy old woman, but as a religious specialist whose role as a mediator between the sacred and profane realms was clearly defined by the tradition of Japanese folk religion. Her eccentric behavior was no longer viewed as a sign of madness, but as proof of her deep spirituality and access to sacred power. Nao was once again permitted to move about freely and had soon gathered about her a small number of devoted followers through her success at faith healing, exorcism, and divination.

In Japanese folk religion, *kamigakari* traditionally served as a form of spontaneous initiation into certain shamanistic roles. The kind of *kamigakari* considered most genuine was one characterized by violent movements and loud animal sounds (Blacker, 1976:277). In other words, the wild, non-human quality of the trance state contributed to its legitimacy as a true religious experience. The violent and prolonged states of *kamigakari* experienced by the founders of most new religions therefore enabled them to establish themselves as religious practitioners. Their new religious identity was acknowledged by the community because their behavior conformed to cultural expectations and could be explained in terms of traditional categories of sacred experience. *Kamigakari* was an immediately recognizable sign of their potential access to and control of sacred power. I say potential because a wild possession experience in itself testified only to the spirit's power and not the medium's. As we just saw

An original passage from Nao's Ofudesaki

in Nao's case, her role as a mediator of Ushitora-no-Konjin's power was not acknowledged until she was able to regulate her states of *kamigakari*. It was only her return to normal behavior following a complete loss of self-control that provided proof of her own power. In this sense, Nao's credibility derived on the one hand from the extremely violent character of her initial trance states and on the other hand from her eventual ability to control the power manifested in her *kamigakari*.

Shimazono Susumu has described a similar pattern in the careers of Nakayama Miki and Kawate Bunjirō, founders respectively of Tenrikyō and Konkōkyō. He points out that "the physically demanding trances of their early periods gave way to more subdued trance states... In some cases there was then no clear indication of any trance state whatever" (Shimazono, 1979:396). In this way, any distinction between the waking (profane) and trance (sacred) states was soon obscured. Paradoxically, this return to normal behavior did not invalidate Miki's and Bunjiro's claims to spiritual power but further reinforced it. In fact, the two founders were thought to exist in a permanent state of divine inspiration and were regarded by their followers as "living *kami*."

This shift, therefore, from a spontaneous and wild form of *kamigakari* to a calm and controlled trance state was necessary to the establishment of a new social and religious identity. Although the unconventional behavior associated with the initial possession experience attracted the community's attention and indicated the relative power of the possessing spirit, only complete self-control and an attitude of inner calm and strength enabled the founder of a new religion to achieve the status of religious practitioner. The founders, in effect, had to learn how to become mediums for the spirits. Anthropologists and psychologists who have studied possession phenomena in other cultures view this process as a common characteristic of spirit mediumship:

> It is only the initial possession state that is often characterized by wild, frenetic actions and complete loss of mental control. When the possession state is studied in one individual over time, his mastery over his kinetic and verbal behavior may be seen to improve significantly... The onset of the trance becomes less abrupt and, if desired, he learns to become a medium for the spirits. This learning process leads to an ability of cult leaders who have practiced the trance state over a long period of time, to be possessed by a spirit which speaks through them and simultaneously to be consciously aware of the

possession -- although this awareness does not seem to negate the validity of the possession experience (Shambaugh, 1978:15).

Kamigakari represented a broad category of psychological and religious experience which was theoretically open to anyone: shamanistic roles were not hereditary. Within its parameters there was room for almost unlimited variation. For example, many of the phenomena defined by modern Western medicine as psychopathological were attributed to spirit possession. As a result of this "open-endedness," the value and meaning assigned to a particular incident of *kamigakari* derived almost entirely from social consensus rooted in specific religious traditions and cultural expectations. Clearly, the presence or absence of this element of "control" was the standard the community used to distinguish a newly initiated shaman from a mentally deranged individual. In his exhaustive study of Japanese shamanism, Sakurai Tokutarō confirms this hypothesis, arguing that what distinguishes the shaman from other religious practitioners and laymen who spontaneously experience *kamigakari* is his or her ability to enter a state of possession (trance) at will (1977:442,492). Once controlled, self-induced *kamigakari* becomes the shaman's particular technique for mediating between gods and humans.

This initial conformity to the traditional role of spiritual medium has led scholars like Hori Ichirō (1968) and Carmen Blacker (1976) to argue that the founders of the new religions are manifestations of the shamanistic tradition characteristic of Japanese folk religion. As we have seen, this is certainly true; however, the initial adoption of a traditional shamanistic role was only the first phase of a founder's career as a religious practitioner. The benefits provided by such customary status were soon outweighed by the constraints it placed on the founders' efforts to achieve their religious goals. Eventually they were forced to expand their beliefs and practices far beyond those of a traditional shaman. If we are to understand the dynamic character and creative potential of the founder's role, we must look more closely at the ways in which it differed from that of a traditional shaman. The major source of these differences lies in a characteristic of *kamigakari* which is generally overlooked by scholars of Japanese religion: as a religious experience, *kamigakari* is not only a mode of behavior associated with the release of formerly repressed emotions; it is also a cognitive process through which prevailing models of reality may be expressed or new ones constructed.

In an unpublished paper on the relationship between altered states of consciousness[5] and culture, Cynthia Shambaugh (1978) presents a model for the analysis of spirit possession and trance which focuses precisely on this creative function. Possession, she argues, represents a transition from one state of consciousness to another. Thus, while entranced, the individual has direct access to a state of consciousness which differs from that of his or her everyday life. Indeed, each of these states of consciousness may be said to have its own "state-specific knowledge." The knowledge associated with the state of trance is organized according to different principles and can provide, therefore, an understanding of reality which differs from that of the waking state. This altered state of consciousness certainly allows for the expression of previously repressed or unconscious emotions and aspirations, but to be meaningful, these emotions as well as the new knowledge revealed in the trance state must be translated into forms comprehensible in the waking state -- that is, to oneself and to others (Shambaugh, 1978:14-17). Symbols, both verbal and nonverbal, constitute the language of this inherently interpretive process -- a process which is necessarily (and at many levels) a dialectical one. Altered states of consciousness represent, therefore, the interaction between the psychological and sociocultural domains, between personal experience and public conceptions and structures. Symbols of course shape experience, but experience also can infuse symbols with new meaning and thus greater validity and relevance.

Victor Turner has argued that symbolic ritual activity is not merely expressive of certain key values and cultural categories, but also has a creative function: "it actually creates, or recreates, the categories through which men perceive reality -- the axioms underlying the structure of society and the laws of the natural and moral orders" (1968:6-7). Shambaugh's claim that the practice of spirit possession in most cultures is best viewed as a cognitive process whereby "models of reality are constantly constructed, revised, and discarded," (1978:16) allows us to characterize *kamigakari* as just such a mode of symbolic activity.

This interpretive framework for the analysis of *kamigakari* contributes in a number of ways to our understanding of the new religions,

---

[5] Shambaugh and Zaretsky (1978:xiii-xiv) have defined "altered states of consciousness" as "mental states...which can be recognized subjectively by the individual himself (or by an objective observer of the individual) as representing a sufficient alteration in subjective experience of psychological functioning from an identifiable state of consciousness previously experienced by that individual."

for it enables us to integrate the psychological and social experiences of a specific individual with his or her projection of a new vision of reality meaningful to others. Other interpretations, like the psychopathological one of Carmen Blacker (1976) or the psychoanalytic one employed by Yasumaru Yoshio (1977) in his biography of Deguchi Nao fail to achieve this integration of the psychological and sociocultural domains. Both discussions leave us wondering how Nao's expression of her darkest thoughts and deepest desires could possibly be understood by others as a coherent and powerfully valid new view of the world. However, if *kamigakari* is seen as a dialectical, cognitive process in which private experience is made meaningful through symbols which are inherently public, but which in turn are given new connotations, new significance, in the context of that private experience, then this link is no longer problematic -- the experience of *kamigakari* itself, as a creative symbolic process, is a form of mediation between an individual and culture. This approach thus leads us from a consideration of the life of a unique individual to an analysis of the broader cultural and social implications of the world view which is projected. What assumptions, concerns, and aspirations informed Nao's construction of a new vision of reality? What kind of symbols did she appropriate and how are they reconstituted and reorganized within the framework of her world view? Finally, who is Nao speaking for? Who shared her assumptions and aspirations and how did her world view meaningfully restructure their experience? This approach enables us, in other words, to address the problem of a popular consciousness.

In this respect, it is the founders' total commitment to a new vision of reality discovered in an altered state of consciousness which most distinguishes them from traditional Japanese mediums. As Shambaugh has pointed out, at the end of trance "the individual is left with two alternatives: to forget the perhaps threatening content of the experience or to integrate that content into, and thereby reformulate, his perception of himself" (1978:14). Traditional mediums followed the former route. They were not conscious of what they said while in a state of trance, nor could they recall the content of the experience after awakening (Sakurai, 1974: 219-220). Although they had learned to control the possession state, their identity as religious practitioners did not derive from a belief in the knowledge provided by that altered state of consciousness, but from their fulfillment of certain social and cultural expectations. In other words, traditional mediums did not tap the creative powers latent in their experience of *kamigakari* in the same way that the founders of the new religions did: they did not construct new, all-encompassing models of reality, but reaffirmed parts of prevailing ones. The reference point for their belief and practice was the established world view and, accordingly, the content of their trance states had only integrative value. They used their new insights to make their clients' experiences meaningful within the context of customary values and social categories, thereby supporting the status quo. Their goal was to change their clients' behavior and attitudes rather than the sociocultural order. Concerned with providing their clients with immediate benefits and relief, their practice contributed to social solidarity.

For those individuals who eventually founded one of the new religions, however, *kamigakari* represented a fundamental conversion experience. Not only did they recall the knowledge revealed to them in a state of trance, but they reformulated their conception of themselves and the world in terms of it. As we have seen, the founders first acquired their identity as religious practitioners by conforming to cultural expectations: *kamigakari* was, after all, a socially sanctioned mode of religious behavior. However, their commitment to the content of their *kamigakari* allowed them to define their religious and social identity not with reference to established religious traditions or social norms, but as an integral part of the new vision of reality revealed to them in an altered state of consciousness.

Deguchi Nao, for example, interpreted her *kamigakari* as the manifestation of an alien consciousness whose presence she had to accept in order to "control" her experience of spirit possession. She finally did this by identifying the alien consciousness as the supreme *kami* in the universe, Ushitora-no-Konjin, and submitting herself to his absolute authority. Thus, what outsiders perceived as self-control was understood subjectively as complete belief in, and total obedience to, this *kami*. She identified herself as the instrument for the communication and realization of this *kami*'s will. Believing that she alone had been chosen as the *kami*'s mouthpiece in the present world, her sense of self-worth was immeasurably enhanced. Deguchi Nao was no longer a nobody, a failure by society's standards, but a very special person with an important mission to carry out -- because she alone had access to the truth, she alone could save the world. It was in fact Nao's low social status and life of hardship that qualified her for this new role. Nao's interpretation of the content of her *kamigakari* thus gave new meaning to her life, both past and present, and transformed her from the victim of uncontrollable social forces to the primary actor in a plan to change the world.

It is this sense of mission, derived from an experience of *kamigakari*, which underlies the active and constructive character of the role of founder in the new religions. It was imperative, given the founders' absolute faith in what they believed to be the revelations of a supremely powerful deity, that they strive to communicate the truth to others and work for the establishment of a new sacred community. A founder's belief in his or her unique role and sacred mission was thus both the source of a new identity and a call to action -- action which was on the one hand informed by, and accordingly expressive of, the vision of reality projected, but which at the same time served to define more clearly the content, structure, and meaning of that vision. As the founders consciously directed their creative energies toward the articulation and actualization of this new vision of reality, they infused customary religious roles, beliefs, and practices with new meaning and redefined the boundaries of religious action as well as their own place within that ever-expanding sphere.

Faith healing and (perhaps paradoxically) *kamigakari* itself are examples of two traditional shamanistic practices which the founders of the new religions appropriated and transformed. Although Nao achieved her own salvation through an experience of *kamigakari*, she prescribed a different route for her followers. Salvation for them lay in repentance and obedience to the will of Ushitora-no-Konjin. It was not that Nao denied that spirit possession and communication with supernatural beings were still possible, but that such communications were no longer necessary and could even be dangerous. The fact that Nao had already revealed the truth precluded the validity of future revelations, for given the unique and absolute character of her own *kamigakari*, the *kamigakari* of others could only reveal false or, at best, partial truths. In this way, Nao circumscribed the traditionally open-ended practice of *kamigakari* while at the same time assigning it new powers. *Kamigakari* now represented not only a source of miscellaneous insights and immediate benefits, but also a source of a total and radically new view of the world and the individual's relationship to the sacred.

Like most of the founders of the new religions, Nao earned a reputation as a successful faith healer quite early in her career. Although we have no firsthand, detailed accounts of her methods, on the basis of scattered references in the *Ofudesaki* and studies of contemporary faith healing practices in Ōmoto (Offner and Van Straelen, 1963), it can at least be said that her techniques were essentially informed by her new vision of reality in terms of which she interpreted her patients' sufferings. Poverty, natural calamities, and disease were all seen as proof of the evil state into which the world, as well as the individual, had fallen. They were signs from the spirit world that people must repent and correct their evil ways. Nao told her patients that their suffering would be relieved only if they had faith in Ushitora-no-Konjin and devoted their lives to the realization of his plan to establish a sacred community on earth. For Nao, the only real cure was salvation through conversion.

In Japanese folk religion, faith healing[6] traditionally served a conservative function. A cure was achieved through the reaffirmation of traditional values and cultural categories and the reintegration of the patient into the established social structure. In this respect, many anthropologists have suggested that faith healing provides a ritual context for the expression and clarification of a cultural system. The healer reconstitutes or reorganizes the disrupted experience of the patient with reference to a specific classificatory system. He or she assigns the patient, as well as the illness, a meaningful place within a sociocultural framework which is thereby articulated and reaffirmed. As Lévi-Strauss has argued, "in contrast with scientific explanation, the problem (in healing rituals) is not to attribute confused and disorganized states, emotions, or representations to an objective cause, but rather to articulate them into a whole system," (1963:182). The shamanistic healer, in other words, explains the inexplicable and objectifies the subjective. He or she provides the patient with "a language by means of which unexpressed and otherwise inexpressible psychic states can be immediately expressed" (1963:198).

Unlike traditional mediums who articulated and structured the experience of their patients in terms of prevailing models of reality, however, the founders of the new religions made their patients' experiences meaningful in terms of the new vision of reality which they were constructing. A successful cure could result, therefore, in the dissociation of the individual from the established sociocultural system. The patient was instead converted to the founder's new world view and integrated into a new community of fellow believers. The founders thus expanded the function of faith healing far beyond the provision of immediate benefits. They used it as a highly effective means of proselytization, for it enabled them to communicate a new view of the world by making it meaningful with regard to an individual's unique experience. Whereas Nao was converted as a result of her *kamigakari*, her followers were often converted through faith healing rituals. In this respect, faith healing derives much of its persuasive power from the translation of personal experiences and emotions into shared symbols. Like *kamigakari*, it represents a creative form of symbolic ritual activity which the founders appropriated and redirected. A cure validated not only the founders' access to sacred power, but demonstrated the truth

---

[6] The popular term for faith healing and the one most often used by the new religions even today is *byōki-naoshi*. The scholarly term is *shinkō chiryō*.

of their revelations, thereby reaffirming their religious legitimacy in the eyes of their followers while at the same time recruiting new members. It is perhaps this complex of factors which scholars have in mind when they attribute a founder's "charisma" to his or her success as a faith healer.[7] Thus, faith healing was not only an effective means of proselytization, but in addition provided the founders with an opportunity to further articulate and systematize the content of their revelations and represent their beliefs in concrete ritual actions.

The knowledge revealed to the founders in an altered state of consciousness also gave them the power and authority to transform established sociocultural structures. Whereas traditional shamans were bound to the prevailing social and cultural system which authorized their religious practices, the founders of the new religions owed allegiance only to a single supreme deity whose will they alone could reveal. Their submission to a transcendent authority actually freed them from their former subjection to the established social and religious authorities. For the founders, the only source of legitimate belief and action was the new world view they had discovered through an experience of *kamigakari*. This total reorientation and concomitant independence from prevailing structures placed them in a position from which they could criticize the sociocultural order and call for a new kind of society.[8] Their construction of a new world view which negated the legitimacy of the present order enabled the founders of the new religions to transform themselves and their followers from objects in the ideological maps of a ruling elite to the subjects of religious ideologies which centered on their own concerns and aspirations.

In this regard, their newly-acquired knowledge represented a potentially dangerous form of power. By locating the source of ultimate authority outside prevailing structures, in the sacred rather than the profane realm, and naming themselves as the sole mouthpiece of that authority, the founders clearly defined what constituted true knowledge and who had access to that truth. The fact that this knowledge was revealed to them through a customary experience of divine inspiration further reinforced its validity. Theirs was not the knowledge of ordinary human beings, but

---

[7] "Charismatic" is a term often used to describe the founders of the new religions. See, for example, Blacker (1976), Hori (1968), and Offner and Van Straelen (1963). It should be remembered, however, that charisma is not an innate human quality, but the result of specific cultural and social processes (Worsely, 1968).

[8] For a discussion of a similar phenomenon among Christian converts in the early Meiji period, see Scheiner (1970).

knowledge which came straight from a supremely powerful deity. It was not conventional knowledge which was partial, particular, and often false, but the total and absolute truth. One could not understand this knowledge just by studying it -- one must believe in it, have faith in it, and put it into practice in one's daily life.

It is often said that the new religions lack any formal doctrine, yet one should not assume that they have nothing to say about human nature, the world, and the relationship between the sacred and profane. To the contrary, the founders had conceptions of the ideal human being and of the world that they wanted desperately to communicate. Similarly, although one is forced to agree with scholars like Hori Ichiro (1968:223) that the founders' social criticism lacked sophistication and specificity, one should not therefore conclude that such criticism is irrelevant to our understanding of the new religions. I would argue, rather, that the critical perspective and transformative leverage inherent in the world views of the founders are centrally important elements of the new religions. Informing the utopian character of their world views and social criticism is a basic affirmation of a notion of sacred community which they consciously opposed to their perception of the established social order.[9] The tendency to underestimate the importance of this aspect of the new religions stems in part from the assumption that a conflicting vision of reality can only be represented in systematic intellectual discourse and achieved through organized political activity. Such a narrow conception of political or ideological dissent naively excludes the obvious power of religious revelation and ritual to create, communicate and affirm a new vision of reality -- a vision which, however vague or enigmatic, may still constitute a threat to the legitimacy and authority of prevailing ideologies.

The role of *kamigakari* in the careers of the founders was thus a very important one. On the one hand, the experience of spirit possession and divine inspiration established a link with traditional beliefs and practices which allowed the founders to assume a religious role and acquire initial legitimacy. At the same time, however, the experience of an altered state of consciousness provided a gap in the sociocultural framework within which the creation of new models of reality was possible. In this way, the founders' commitment to the world view discovered in an experience of *kamigakari* ultimately enabled them to break with traditional social and religious forms and to construct new ones.

---

[9] See Harootunian (1982), for a more detailed discussion of the new religions as "ideologies of conflict."

II
Experience and Consciousness:
The Historical Context

The argument that *kamigakari* as a transformative and creative experience is in large part responsible for the special character of the new religions raises an important question: what factors induce an individual to experience such an altered state of consciousness and grant such great significance to the knowledge revealed therein? More specifically, how do we account for Nao's sudden leap, at the age of fifty-five, into an altered state of consciousness and her complete commitment to the new vision of reality it provided? The answer is necessarily a complex one, for it involves emotional, cognitive, and sociocultural factors, all of which are embedded in a specific historical context. Accordingly, in addressing these questions, this chapter includes an examination of the relevant aspects of the larger sociocultural order in late nineteenth century Japan as well as a discussion of Nao's life history and her efforts to establish an independent cult based on her experience of *kamigakari*. I have chosen this approach because I am convinced that it is only through an historical analysis sensitive to the dialectical relationship between consciousness and socioeconomic circumstances on the one hand and religion and politics on the other that the content and structure of Nao's world view, and especially its ideological significance, can be understood. This chapter thus lays the necessary historical and theoretical foundation for the analysis of Nao's religious teachings and writings which follows in Chapter III.

The Life of Deguchi Nao

In focusing on the life history of this remarkable woman, it is not my intention to reduce the world view she constructed to a mere reflection of her unique experience and private concerns, but to deepen our understanding of that world view and establish its broader social and political implications. There are two ways, therefore, in which the relevance of Nao's life history to the analysis of the religion she founded goes far beyond the introductory function generally attributed to such biographies. First, Nao arrived at her new vision of reality through the reinterpretation of her own past: the concerns and assumptions that informed her construction of that vision as well as the raw materials from which it was constructed are grounded in her personal history. This dialectical relationship between her religious doctrine and personal experience manifests itself even in the undifferentiated form of her writings. Nao did not write separate memoirs, but included her reflections on her past and present experience in her *Ofudesaki*.[10] There, scattered amidst religious revelations, eschatological predictions, and social criticism, one finds her recollections of and commentaries on her own life. Whereas scholars draw their ideas from the body of classical and contemporary texts available to them, Nao drew hers from her experience in, and perceptions of, the society around her, both of which were structured by the prevailing system of Japanese folk religious belief and popular morality.

Second, in order to determine the historicity of Nao's world view and the ways in which it could have been meaningful to others, we must locate her within the larger social structure and identify the social group whose perception of reality she shared. In this respect, Nao's life history allows us to identify her with a class of people dislocated and oppressed by the rapid socioeconomic changes that Japan underwent in the late nineteenth century. In addition, it enables us to characterize a way of life and, more importantly, a way of thinking about life, rarely documented in histories of the Meiji Period -- the experience and consciousness of the "commoners," especially women, who did not share in the government's ideology of progress through modernization.

Much of what is known about Nao's life has been culled from her own writings.[11] This dependence on autobiographical sources has both advantages and disadvantages. On the one hand, as Yasumaru Yoshio has warned, in looking back on her life from the perspective of one who has

---

[10] When Onisaburō edited the *Ofudesaki* for publication, he omitted many of the passages in which Nao wrote about her own life. This version of the *Ofudesaki*, called the *Ōmoto shinyu*, is now one of Ōmoto's sacred texts. In 1973, however, a group of scholars conducting a study of Ōmoto collected Nao's autobiographical writings and published them as the *Keireki no shinyu*.

[11] Another important source of our information about Nao's life is her daughter Sumi's memoirs which were published in 1955 under the title *Osanagatari*.

since experienced great unhappiness and a profound religious conversion, Nao no doubt transformed the meaning that certain events originally had for her (1977:29). On the other hand, autobiographical sources seem especially conducive to the analysis of consciousness, for however dramatized or distorted Nao's account of her life may be, it still provides important clues to her basic values, beliefs, and aspirations. Consequently, it is appropriate to be more concerned with the assumptions and interests informing Nao's reconstruction and interpretation of her life than with the objective reality of her recollections.

Nao was born in the winter of 1837 in Fukuchiyama, a bustling castle town northwest of Kyoto on the Yura River.[12] Her grandfather, an official carpenter of the domain, was allowed to carry a sword and use a surname, honors at that time usually reserved for samurai. The financial security and relatively high social status which he acquired for his family did not last, however. Nao's father, Kirimura Gorosaburō, accustomed to the easy life of his youth and given to squandering his time and money on frequent drunken binges, lacked the training and discipline required of a successful artisan and was unable to maintain the family's position and wealth. In the years following Nao's birth, the Kirimuras' situation gradually declined and they found themselves among the ranks of Fukuchiyama's semi-employed city poor: in order to support their four children, Gorosaburō peddled sweet rice wine and his wife, Soyo, made cotton thread at home. When Nao was nine years old, her father participated in a pilgrimage to Ise (Yasumaru, 1977:21). Shortly after returning home, he was stricken with a severe illness and died a few months later. The widowed Soyo, unable to care for the family by herself, sent Nao out to work in one of the large merchant households in Fukuchiyama.

It was not uncommon at that time for young girls from poorer families to find employment in the households of wealthy relatives, neighbors, or local merchants. Because most of these young women, like Nao, gave their meager earnings to their parents, such employment represented an additional source of income for their families. The girls, meanwhile, received not only room and board, but training in various domestic and occupational skills as well. As was the custom, therefore, Nao lived with her employer's family. During the day, she helped with the cooking and cleaning or worked in the store. She spent her evenings

---

[12] Nao's birth date of December 16, 1836, is reckoned according to the lunar calendar. According to the solar calendar, however, she was born on January 22, 1837. I have used the latter date to calculate Nao's age throughout this book.

spinning thread and stringing coins. Nao was employed by four different merchants in her six years of service. Two ran dry goods and dressmaking shops; the others made *manjū* (steamed buns filled with jam). Nao's honesty, diligence, and devotion to her mother impressed her employers: in her third year of service, she was awarded a prize as one of Fukuchiyama's most filial daughters (Yasumaru, 1977:24).

Nao finally returned home in the fall of her fifteenth year. She helped her mother with the household chores and worked in nearby silk reeling factories during the summer. When she was eighteen, Nao moved to Ayabe, a town about twenty miles east of Fukuchiyama, to marry Deguchi Masagorō. Nao's marriage to this man, the adopted heir of her maternal aunt, Deguchi Yuri, crushed all her youthful hopes for happiness. The circumstances which finally compelled her to enter a marriage she initially opposed reveal important aspects of Nao's character and religious beliefs.

The Deguchi family, when Nao's aunt Yuri married into it, was one of the three wealthiest households in Ayabe. Although her husband, the adopted heir, lost some of the family fortune, Yuri was still very well off at the time of his death in 1846: in addition to her two-story home and large warehouse, she owned a great deal of land (Yasumaru, 1977:27). Yuri, who had no children of her own, was very lonely after her husband's death and soon became involved in a scandalous love affair with a man she had known before her marriage. Her elder brother and brother-in-law took advantage of her weakened social position and financial naiveté and tried to embezzle her inheritance. Fearing the extinction of the family line as well as the family fortune, Yuri adopted Nao in 1853 (Yasumaru, 1977:28).

Nao, who was then sixteen years old, at first grudgingly agreed to the adoption and went to live with her aunt in Ayabe. It soon became clear that Yuri intended to adopt a husband for Nao and, by naming the two as her legitimate heirs, ensure the continuation of the Deguchi household or *ie*. Nao, however, had a change of heart and stubbornly refused to go along with her aunt's plans. After less than six months in Ayabe, she returned home (Yasumaru, 1977:28).

Nao's recalcitrance is not difficult to understand. Certainly, her uncles' insidious behavior and her aunt's clandestine lifestyle clashed with Nao's strict moral sense. But just as importantly, Nao had fallen in love with a young man from a village near Fukuchiyama. The two had already spoken of marriage and hoped to one day open a small store together (Yasumaru, 1977:29). It took more than gentle requests or even tearful pleas to persuade the strong-willed Nao to abandon this dream and subject herself instead to the troubles of the declining Deguchi family.

Several months after Nao's departure, Yuri went to visit her in Fukuchiyama. The anger and despair in her manner frightened Nao and her mother. Yuri expressed intense hatred for her brothers and begged Nao to return to Ayabe and marry Masagorō. She was afraid that if Nao did not succeed her in the Deguchi household, there would be no one to care for the family ancestral spirits. Yuri's final words were not a desperate appeal, however, but a malicious threat. In a chilling voice, she said of her brothers, "After I die I am going to haunt them and I will not be satisfied until I have trapped them in sewer pots and burned them to ashes!" That night, Yuri drowned herself in a well near her lover's house (Yasumaru, 1977:28).

A few days after Yuri's suicide, Nao developed a high fever and fell into a deep coma. When she later recovered, she attributed her sudden, severe illness to Yuri's spirit, which had appeared before her the night she became sick demanding to know why she had not yet gone to Ayabe (Yasumaru, 1977: 28). The consequences of Nao's refusal to obey Yuri had now taken on a more immediate and alarming character -- if Nao did not take responsibility for the Deguchi ancestral shrine, there would be no one to properly care for and thus appease her aunt's vengeful spirit, a spirit which had, moreover, shown itself capable of harming Nao herself. Compelled as much by her fear of Yuri's spirit as her own sense of duty, Nao returned to Ayabe in the spring of 1855 and married Deguchi Masagorō (Yasumaru, 1977:32).

Nao's fear of the potentially malevolent power of her dead aunt and her resulting compliance with Yuri's wishes are best viewed in the context of Japanese folk belief, for it was a commonly held notion that the spirits of the dead could, and often did, affect the living. In particular, the spirits of the newly dead, called *shirei*, who had not yet severed their ties with the world of the living, were thought to be the ones most likely to interfere in the affairs of their former relatives and neighbors. The *shirei* of an individual who had died a violent death, such as suicide, or in a state of intense jealousy, rage, or bitterness, was believed to constitute an even greater threat: seeking their just retribution, such troubled souls inevitably returned to settle their accounts with the living (Smith, 1974:41,44). It was thus not uncommon for sudden illness or seemingly undeserved misfortunes to be attributed to an angry *shirei*. Unless propitiated and purified with the proper rites, these *shirei* would never find peace as guardian ancestral spirits (*sorei*), but would wander the earth in a state of eternal torment, wreaking havoc upon the living. In some cases, when even the proper rituals failed to appease the vengeful *shirei*, the victims of its wrath would try to fulfill the person's last request or somehow right the injustices he or she had suffered while alive.

Yuri's intense hatred and tragic suicide undoubtedly qualified her for the role of an angry *shirei*. In order to free Yuri from endless torment and herself from Yuri's rage, Nao had no choice but to accept responsibility for the Deguchi ancestral shrine. Nao's world, like her memoirs, was peopled by a myriad of spiritual beings, benevolent, malevolent, and benign, as well as beings of a decidedly more earthly character. In the world view of the Japanese folk, a view that Nao clearly shared, the physical and spiritual realms constituted not separate but overlapping categories: there were no clear lines drawn between the living and the dead, the human and the divine.

When Nao married Masagorō,[13] he was twenty-eight years old. She and her daughter Sumi describe him as a cheerful, easygoing fellow who never worried about what the future might bring. An irrepressible clown, Masagorō preferred to play with the neighborhood children or joke with his friends over a bottle of sake than to work. This carefree man was thus the antithesis of Nao, whose natural austerity and reticence, unflagging diligence, and moral rigidity only intensified as she grew older. Confronted with her husband's irresponsible behavior, Nao would lapse into stubborn, self-righteous silence. But Masagorō, never able to take anything seriously, would merely chide her in his usual lighthearted manner, "If you keep your mouth shut like that, worms will grow in it!"[14] Each was a constant source of aggravation for the other.

For the first several years of their marriage, Nao and Masagorō were actually quite well-to-do. They owned the large house and agricultural land which they had inherited from Yuri and Masagorō, who was a skilled carpenter, earned a substantial income through the construction contracts that he and his three apprentices received. As early as 1860, however, their financial situation and social status had begun to decline. Masagorō was very naive about financial matters, a weakness that local money lenders and opportunistic neighbors were quick to take advantage of. Without

---

[13] Before Masagorō was adopted by the Deguchi family, his name was Shikata Toyosuke. He came from a village in what is now the western part of Kyoto-fu.

[14] Quoted in Yasumaru, 1977:34. *"Omae no yō ni sō damatte iru to, kuchi no naka ni mushi ga waku wai naa."*

consulting Nao, he sold almost all of their property. Later, when Nao discovered what he had done, he cheerfully confessed that he had spent all the money on sake (Yasumaru, 1977:36). Unfortunately, an unquenchable thirst for sake was another one of Masagorō's weaknesses and as the years passed, he spent more and more of his time drinking. He eventually lost interest in his work and became sloppy and careless. As a result, his reputation as a carpenter, which had once aroused the bitter jealousy of other carpenters in Ayabe, sank so low as to arouse only their laughter and scorn. He received so few contracts that he could no longer afford to keep apprentices and Nao had to help him with the heavy work (Yasumaru, 1977:38).

In 1872, in order to pay off their debts, Nao and Masagorō were forced to sell their home. It must have been a difficult decision, for the house had been in the Deguchi family for generations. After living for six months in the small storehouse in the backyard, they sold that, too, and moved into a rented house in another part of Ayabe. By this time the Deguchis had five children. The two oldest had already left home: Yone, sixteen, was employed by a family in Ayabe and Koto, ten, was living with Nao's brother in Fukuchiyama. The youngest child was only one year old. Seemingly overwhelmed by their misfortunes, Masagoro avoided all responsibility. If he was not wandering aimlessly through the streets, his carpentry tools wrapped in an old towel and flung over his shoulder, then he could be found in one of the neighborhood taverns, drinking himself into blissful oblivion (Yasumaru, 1977:38). Because her husband was contributing so little to support the family, this responsibility fell primarily on Nao's shoulders. Not one to complain, and certainly not one to give up, she quietly and diligently persevered. Drawing on the skills she had acquired as a young servant in Fukuchiyama, Nao opened a small restaurant. When that didn't work out, she made and sold *manjū* (Yasumaru, 1977:38).

In 1876, Nao and Masagorō built a small house on the only piece of land they still owned. Masagorō had purchased the property, adjacent to their first home, from the village years ago. No one else was interested in the land for it was believed to be cursed. Nao and Masagorō did all of the construction work themselves. Carrying hundreds of stones from the nearby river, they even built a new well. At the entrance to the house was a small room with a wooden floor where Nao could sell her *manjū*. Behind it were the two *tatami* (straw mats used as floor coverings) rooms where the family lived. Nao built two small shelves, or altars, on the south wall. On one (the *butsudan*) she placed the Deguchi family ancestral tablets. The other (*kamidana*) was used to worship a variety of Shinto and folk deities. Nao lived in this house until 1893; during her first *kamigakari*, she used the well they had dug in the backyard to perform her cold water ablutions.

Between the years 1856 and 1882, Nao gave birth to eleven children, three of whom died in infancy. The eldest was born when Nao was nineteen years old and the youngest when she was forty-five. Supporting this large family and raising the children constituted one of Nao's greatest hardships. Although the Deguchi children remembered their mother as a kind and loving person, they also recalled that she was a harsh disciplinarian. When they misbehaved, Nao did not raise her voice in reprimands but glared at them silently. At such times, her eyes glittered coldly and her expression hardened in anger. The children feared those stern, accusing looks (Yasumaru, 1977:40-41). The Deguchi children, especially the older ones who had spent their early years in relative comfort and economic security, were perhaps unable to meet the demands of their strong-willed, self-righteous mother who worked so hard and suffered so uncomplainingly -- and expected her children to do the same. Nao was, after all, well-acquainted with poverty. As a child herself she had known little else. Her father, like her children's father, had preferred drinking sake to working. Nao, no doubt, expected her children to deal with these unfortunate circumstances as she had -- with filial devotion and diligence. Although the younger ones did try to conform to her expectations, the older children could not and eventually rebelled against their mother.

Nao's first-born, Yone, had always been an obedient child and a great help to her mother, but when she was nineteen she shocked her parents by leaving the husband they had chosen for her and running away with a local gangster, Ōtsuki Shikazō, who was seventeen years her senior. The couple soon returned to Ayabe, however, and opened the town's first butcher shop. It proved to be a very successful business, but Nao, utterly scandalized by the incident, would have nothing to do with her nouveau riche daughter for many years (Yasumaru, 1977:41-42). Even after their reconciliation, their relationship was a tense one. Nao believed that her daughter and son-in-law were too concerned with making money and stubbornly refused to accept any assistance from them. After her *kamigakari*, Nao tried to persuade the couple to repent so that their material wealth could be used to help realize Ushitora-no-Konjin's divine plan and thus acquire positive value (Yasumaru, 1977:148). In Nao's *Ofudesaki*, Yone and Shikazō are often represented as the personification of evil in a world which places too much value on money (Yasumaru, 1977:77).

Yone's urge to escape was shared by two of her siblings. Nao's second daughter, Koto, also ran away from home when she was nineteen. Takezō, the Deguchis' eldest son, was a spoiled, sickly young man who shunned hard work and responsibility. His parents tried to apprentice him to a carpenter, but, complaining about his poor health and the terrible food, he quit and returned home (Yasumaru, 1977:44). Later, while apprenticed to a second carpenter, he tried unsuccessfully to commit suicide and was sent home to recuperate. When he had recovered, Nao insisted that he go back to work, but the twenty-two year old Takezō instead fled from Ayabe and did not return until 1903 (Yasumaru, 1977:46-47).

Nao's second son, Seikichi, was her favorite and she hoped that he would one day assume the headship of the Deguchi family. It was the quiet, obedient Seikichi who walked daily through the streets of Ayabe, selling the *manjū* which Nao so painstakingly made to support her household. Seikichi was apprenticed to a local paper maker and eventually opened his own shop with the help of his brother-in-law. At the age of twenty, however, he was drafted into the army and three years later, in 1895, he died in Taiwan during the Sino-Japanese War. Nao was devastated. Even after Seikichi's remains were sent to her, she continued to believe that he was alive and would one day return to Ayabe to help her with her divine mission (Yasumaru, 1977:149-150).

Nao was also very fond of her third daughter, Hisa, but Hisa left home to marry a man who lived in Yagi, a town that was a full day's walk to the southeast of Ayabe. Hisa's husband, Fukushima Toranosuke, operated a rickshaw, a "modern convenience" (it was invented in 1869) which Nao viewed as an evil influence and later forbade her followers to use. Hisa ran a small tea shop on the main highway outside Yagi which catered to travelers on their way to Kyoto. Like her mother, Hisa had to work to help support her family. After her *kamigakari*, Nao stayed with the Fukushimas while recuperating from her long imprisonment. Hisa and her husband were the first to acknowledge the power of Nao's *kami* and came to number among her most devoted followers (Yasumaru, 1977:109).

Nao's three youngest children were all born after the Deguchis had moved into their new house in 1876. Of these, Denkichi and Ryō figure very little in Nao's memoirs. Sumi, however, Nao's youngest child, was her constant companion and played a primary role in the founding and later development of Ōmotokyō. When Nao became pregnant with Sumi in 1882, she was forty-five years old. Feeling that her condition was shameful for a woman of her age, Nao disguised it by tying her *obi* (a wide cloth sash worn over the *kimono*) very tightly. Her family and neighbors were rather surprised, therefore, when she "suddenly" gave birth to a tiny, but strong and healthy Sumi (Yasumaru, 1977:44). Sumi was a clever, rambunctious child who was always getting into mischief, but she was also devoted to her mother. It was the headstrong, warm-hearted Sumi who ultimately succeeded Nao as head of the Deguchi family (Nao adopted Sumi's husband, Deguchi Onisaburō) and spiritual leader of Ōmotokyō.

In 1884, the Deguchi's long descent into poverty finally ended in bankruptcy. By making and selling *manjū*, however, Nao was able to support the family on a day-to-day basis (Yasumaru, 1977:44). One of Sumi's earliest memories is of Nao sitting before her large stone mortar late at night grinding rice flour for the next day's batch of *manjū* (Deguchi Sumi, 1976:22-23). The following year brought another calamity: the fifty-eight year old Masagorō fell from the roof where he was working and seriously injured his back. The accident left him permanently paralyzed. Nao was forced to take up rag collecting in order to feed her children and bedridden husband. While Hisa, who was then fifteen, cared for her father and younger siblings, Nao went out every day to collect and sell old scraps of cloth.

Rag collecting, or *borokai*, was an occupation that only the very poor ever engaged in. As a means of earning a living it was only a short step above begging, a last resort for those whose destitution had not yet deprived them of their pride (Yasumaru, 1977:45-46). It was also lonely, grueling work. Nao's search for rags would often take her to villages more than seventeen miles from Ayabe. In the winter, traveling after dark, she sometimes lost her way on the snowy mountain paths and would not return home until very late at night, cold, hungry, and exhausted (Yasumaru, 1977:51).

In the summer, Nao tried to find work at nearby silk reeling factories because it was more profitable than rag collecting. Such work required that she be away from home for weeks at a time. Given her husband's condition, this was often impossible. Masagorō, in spite of his completely debilitating illness, never lost his cheerful disposition, but he was more of a burden to Nao than ever before. Seemingly insensitive to his wife's hardships and the family's financial difficulties, he constantly demanded expensive food and, of course, sake. The ever-obedient Nao always tried to get him what he wanted, even if it meant begging her relatives and neighbors for the food he requested or pawning the last of their belongings to buy sake (Yasumaru, 1977:52). Two years after his accident, in 1887, Masagorō died. Immediately following the simple funeral, for which her neighbors had to pay, Nao returned to her silk reeling and rag collecting (Yasumaru, 1977:53). She continued to engage in these occupations until her *kamigakari* five years later.

Certain events in the months preceding Nao's first *kamigakari* in January, 1892, are worth noting because they reveal the extreme emotional and physical stress she was under at the time. They also indicate that Nao had become deeply involved in the phenomenon of spirit possession before her own possession experience.

In 1890, Hisa, shortly after the birth of her first child, had a nervous breakdown. Nao went to Yagi to help care for her. Hisa's husband, believing that his wife's "insanity" had been caused by a malevolent spirit, called in a Konkōkyō practitioner to pray for her. While performing the exorcism ritual, he intoned the name of Ushitora-no-Konjin and afterwards attributed Hisa's rapid recovery to the power of this compassionate *kami*. This was Nao's first contact with Konkōkyō and its central deity who was initially known as Ushitora-no-Konjin. She must have been impressed with the *kami*'s response to their prayers, for when she returned to Ayabe a while later, she enshrined a Konkōkyō amulet in her home (Yasumaru, 1977:79). She would eventually claim, moreover, that it was this same *kami*, Ushitora-no-Konjin, who had possessed her in order to reveal his plan to reconstruct the world.

The following year, Nao's eldest daughter, Yone, also went insane. While making *mochi* (rice cakes) for the upcoming New Year festivities, Yone suddenly flew into a violent rage, overturning the hibachi and kicking utensils around the room. Her husband, Ōtsuki Shikazō, tied her to a post in the house to prevent her from hurting herself (Yasumaru, 1977:75). Between fits of hysteria, Yone tearfully pleaded with her husband to repent and give up his greedy ways. She was also deathly afraid of her mother and cried out that there was a baboon in the room whenever Nao came near her. Although Shikazō, a confirmed skeptic who never took his mother-in-law's moral admonitions or religious beliefs seriously, was convinced that his wife had gone completely mad, Nao insisted that Yone had been possessed by an evil spirit and tried to persuade Shikazō to comply with his wife's request that he reform himself. Yone never recovered her sanity, a tragedy that Nao blamed on Shikazō. Not surprisingly, the *Ofudesaki* often uses Shikazō as an example of the type of person most difficult to convert (Yasumaru, 1977:77).

Nao experienced her first *kamigakari* only a week after the onset of Yone's illness. That morning, although she was exhausted from caring for Yone and anxious about her daughter's condition, Nao went out as usual to collect and sell old rags. Thinking of her trudging along rough, snowy roads, cold and alone, one is reminded of the solitary vision quests of the American Indians or the arduous journeys which mark the initiation of Siberian shamans. It is true that in cultures where spirit possession is commonly acknowledged, extreme physical deprivation and/or psychological stress can spontaneously induce an altered state of consciousness. The latter certainly accounts for Yone's and Hisa's experiences of *kamigakari*. In Nao's case, however, this interpretation alone does not explain the most important aspect of her experience of *kamigakari*: the content and import of the revelations she made while in a state of trance. The problem here seems to be more one of consciousness than immediate physical conditions or psychological disorders. The key to its resolution thus lies in our definition of *kamigakari* as an essentially cognitive experience that allows for the revision or rejection of formerly accepted models of reality and the construction of new ones.

Nao's *kamigakari* represented a profound transformation in her consciousness. After this experience, she saw herself and the world around her in a completely different way. She rejected the validity of the prevailing social order in which, in her view, the strong exploited the weak and money, not moral virtue, was valued and rewarded. Predicting the imminent destruction of this society, she projected a vision of a new divine order, a heaven on earth, to replace it and claimed for herself a pivotal role in its establishment. When we consider these apocalyptic yet self-affirming and utopian revelations from the perspective of Nao's personal history, it becomes clear that an acute awareness of a great discrepancy between what she believed society should be and what it actually was, between her expectations and her experience, informed her leap into an altered state of consciousness.

Although Nao had lived in strict accordance with the morality she had learned as a child, she never achieved the rewards of personal happiness and prosperity that conformity to that ethical code implicitly guaranteed. In spite of her long years of hard work and self-sacrifice, Nao found herself relegated to the lowest status in the social order -- a poverty-stricken widow with no hope of a better future. Too proud to accept society's negative assessment of her worth, Nao instead denied the legitimacy of the social order which had defined her as worthless. Unable to abandon the ethical code which was the source of her personal dignity and integrity, she instead identified it with a religious imperative and made it the basis of her vision of a new divine order. We do not know when Nao first became aware of this conflict between her own values and those of the society at large, for it was only within an altered state of consciousness that she was able to articulate and resolve it. After a lifetime of suffering in silence, Nao finally found in her experience of *kamigakari* a legitimate voice for her anger and an absolute assurance of spiritual salvation and socioeconomic emancipation.

Nao did not speak only for herself, however. To the contrary, her writings are a rare expression of the experience and consciousness common to a class of people oppressed by the social, economic, and legal reforms enacted by the Meiji state. In the *Ofudesaki* Nao voices an anger, a perception of social inequity and moral corruption, and a hope for a better way of life that were widely shared in late nineteenth century Japan.

Conventional Morality and Economic Oppression in Late Nineteenth Century Japan

In order to assert that Nao, through her *kamigakari*, articulated the concerns and aspirations of a social group whose experience and consciousness she shared, we must identify the socioeconomic class she spoke for and the cognitive categories, values, and expectations that constituted its collective consciousness. Lucien Goldmann has argued that "statements cannot be validly studied by separating them from the individual who formulates them or by separating this individual from the socio-historical relations in which he is involved" (1973:112). It is not that the writer merely reflects the collective consciousness in his or her writings, but rather that he or she "advances considerably the degree of structural coherence which the collective consciousness itself has so far attained in only a rough and ready fashion" (1973:115). Goldmann's interpretive approach, which clearly assumes a dialectical relationship between text and context at the level of "deep structure," does not deny the importance of individual creativity but forces us to take into account its inherently sociocultural character. A valid explanation of a text requires, therefore, not only an analysis of its internal coherence, but also the identification of "the collective subject in relation to which the mental structure which governs the work has a functional character" (Goldmann, 1970:588).

In the preceding section, we identified two broad sets of mutually reinforcing assumptions, values, and expectations which structured Nao's interpretation of both her own experience and the larger social order: a conventional moral code and a system of popular religious belief and practice. Together these constitute a comprehensive pattern of norms for action and thought, a way of thinking about the world and one's proper place in it, that was characteristic of a Japanese folk consciousness in the nineteenth century. I have already examined the religious elements of this popular consciousness in my discussion of Nao's marriage and her experience of *kamigakari* and will address them again in subsequent chapters. Here I would like to focus on the code of ethics and social expectations intrinsic to this popular consciousness.

The moral code to which Nao was so deeply committed held up loyalty, obedience, sincerity, and filial piety as the most noble of human virtues and stressed the importance of reverence to one's ancestors and selfless devotion to one's social superiors. It enjoined individuals to strive assiduously to fulfill their familial obligations and sacrifice their personal needs and desires to insure the well-being of the household and the continuation of the family line. It placed a high value on productivity, encouraging frugality and self-discipline while condemning idleness and consumption. Within the framework of this ethical code, the righteous and diligent execution of one's ascribed duties acquired the authority of an absolute moral imperative.

Yasumaru Yoshio has argued that this system of conventional morality, or *tsūzoku dōtoku*, was a synthesis of the ethical and religious teachings of several lay organizations popular in the Tokugawa period: Shingaku, Hōtoku, and Fuji-kō (1977:70). In this respect, it was an ethical code initially articulated for, and practiced by, the ruling classes and powerful merchants (samurai, wealthy townsmen, village administrators, and prosperous peasants) and only later assimilated by the poorer peasants, artisans, and townspeople. The *tsūzoku dōtoku* was tied, moreover, to prevailing social institutions and did not question either the political authority of the state or the legitimacy of the Tokugawa social order. It was thus not only a popular folk ethos, but a powerful and pervasive ideology supportive of established political and social arrangements. A brief discussion of two movements, Shingaku and Hōtoku, which contributed to the formation of the *tsūzoku dōtoku* should help to clarify its content and ideological character.

When Ishida Baigan (1685-1744) founded Shingaku in 1729, the merchant class, despite its ever increasing activity, influence, and wealth, was still excluded from the moral social order formulated by Tokugawa Confucians. Baigan tried to correct this situation by, in effect, creating a "samurai ethic" for the merchant and artisan classes.[15] It was not his

---

[15] For a more detailed discussion of Ishida Baigan and his teachings, see Bellah (1957).

intention to change or even criticize the Tokugawa social order, but to re-evaluate the merchant's place within it. He argued that merchant activity was as necessary to the well-being of the realm, and as moral, as the activity of the samurai. The merchant's profits were not the result of selfish greed, but, like the samurai's stipend, a reward for diligence and self-sacrifice within his appointed occupation. Baigan clearly shared the Confucian view that private desires must be suppressed for the public good, for he placed great importance on selfless devotion to one's occupation or business, loyalty to one's superiors, and filial piety. He prescribed, moreover, an almost ascetic life-style of frugality and diligence. Shingaku represented a powerful fusion of religious and ethical teachings, for Baigan identified the merchant's diligent practice of his proper duties with religious action. In his view it was a means of eliminating private desires and achieving union with the divine.

Shingaku spread rapidly among the merchant and artisan classes throughout Japan and by the nineteenth century had become almost synonymous with the customary ethical code of a popular *chōnin* consciousness. We find this ethical code, for example, in the *kakun*, or household regulations, of late Tokugawa merchant and artisan families. The *kakun* portray service to the family business as a moral and sacred obligation and enjoin family members and employees to be honest, obedient, and above all, diligent (Bellah, 1957:123-124).

The Hōtoku movement, founded in the early nineteenth century by Ninomiya Sontoku (1787-1856), tried to do for the peasants what Shingaku had done for the merchants -- claim a higher status for them in the moral, not the political, order. It, too, soon acquired a large following. Ninomiya wanted to provide the peasants with a practical ethic which would increase agricultural production while giving meaning to their labor. He thus stressed the need for technological improvements as well as the importance of diligence, frugality, and humility.[16] Although Ninomiya acknowledged that increased productivity depended in part on the subjugation of nature, he still insisted that human beings were indebted to nature (or Heaven) as well as the ancestral spirits and should always be grateful for the benefits

---

[16] Many Hōtoku societies were founded in the 1880s, but these, unlike their Tokugawa predecessors, primarily attracted progressive landowners who were interested not in the movement's ethical teachings, but in the agricultural technology and rural industrialization it encouraged and the credit associations it established (Havens, 1974:45). Although Ninomiya's ethical teachings were dropped by his later followers, they persisted in the *tsūzoku dōtoku* of the late nineteenth century.

(*on*) received from it. In his view, diligent labor was the principal means of repaying those debts.

Whereas the religious character of Baigan's teachings seems to be drawn primarily from Neo-Confucian notions of self-cultivation, Ninomiya's teachings, with their emphasis on communal cooperation and the repayment of *on*, seem closer to folk Shinto beliefs and practices. However, both Shingaku and Hōtoku encouraged ancestor worship, a fact closely related to their common assumption that the *ie* (household) was the basic unit of production and consumption in Tokugawa society.

Given its roots in these practical ethical teachings explicitly aimed at the preservation of the household as a religious and economic unit, it is not surprising that the *tsūzoku dōtoku* was also inextricably tied to the notion of the *ie* as an independent family institution. Implicit in this conventional morality was the promise that behavior in accordance with its dictates would result in the prosperity and perpetuation of the *ie* and thus the happiness and security of the individual. According to Yasumaru, this synthesis of personal aspirations, ethical code, and social institution was popularly perceived as an ideal pattern or life cycle which experience was assumed to validate. People expected that their patient, diligent labor would eventually result in the prosperity of their household and thus secure their own happiness (Yasumaru, 1977:71). The identification of the maintenance of one's family line and economic success with personal happiness could inspire conformity to the ethical code while lending purpose and hope to the individual's hard work and self-sacrifice: the guarantee of a better life in the future enabled one to endure the otherwise insufferable present. Reinforced by an economic system that guaranteed the security of the small producer and legitimized by success, this conventional morality served to integrate individuals, through their values, ambitions, and daily labor, into the larger sociocultural system.

Although grounded in Tokugawa ideology, the *tsūzoku dōtoku* continued to be a powerful and pervasive force in Meiji society, just as the perpetuation of the *ie* persisted as a highly valued and ardently pursued goal among people of all classes and occupations. In his study of the Meiji records of a small village in the Kantō region, William Chambliss found that the longevity of its *ie* was still the major determinant of a family's social status. Moreover, the high incidence of adoption which he discovered there (in 1875, eighteen out of a total of fifty household heads were adopted) testifies to the continuing importance placed on the survival of the family line (Chambliss, 1965:40). As an essentially conservative ideology which encouraged self-improvement and productivity within the prescribed limits of the given sociopolitical order, the *tsūzoku dōtoku* was just as well suited to the aims of the Meiji state as it was to the Tokugawa government.

When we speak, therefore, of a "conventional morality" in nineteenth century Japan, we are not merely referring to a simple list of moral injunctions, but to a comprehensive paradigm embodying specific values, assumptions, and aspirations; to a whole way of thinking about the meaning and purpose of life. The *tsūzoku dōtoku* defined a particular vision of reality, structuring action and channeling emotions in politically desirable directions. Yasumaru Yoshio has accordingly argued that the *tsūzoku dōtoku*, by inspiring a spirit of self-discipline, obedience, and economic independence in the Japanese people, supported Japan's transition from a "feudal" to a "modern" society.[17]

There were many, however, like Nao, who never achieved the prosperity and happiness that adherence to the moral tenets of the *tsūzoku dōtoku* was supposed to guarantee. The particular view of social reality that it represented failed to account for the experience of those poorer peasants and townspeople struggling to make a living at a time of rapid socioeconomic change. Meiji fiscal policy and increasing industrialization in the last three decades of the nineteenth century transformed the economic structures which had enabled those clinging to the bottom rungs of the socioeconomic ladder to realize (at least partially) the aspirations implicit in the *tsūzoku dōtoku*. Worse than the poverty itself, as we shall see, was the sudden loss of the means whereby families had formerly been able to improve their financial situation.

In 1873, the Meiji government revised its agricultural tax system and recognized the private ownership of land. Previously based on the percentage of yield (usually forty to fifty percent) and paid in kind, the new monetary tax was set at three percent of the assessed value of the land. This land tax, even when reduced to two and a half percent in 1876, was intentionally heavy, for the government did not want to impose unnecessary burdens on the development of trade and industry. In 1880, the land tax accounted for four-fifths of all tax revenues (Fairbank, et al., 1965:235).

This tax reform had a devastating impact on the "marginal peasant" (those with very small land holdings, tenant farmers, and those dependent on other non-agricultural forms of employment) and contributed

---

[17] Yasumaru Yoshio, 1977:70. This is also a central theme of his *Nihon no kindaika to minshū shisō*.

directly to the dispossession of the peasantry and the increase in tenancy. In his study of Chiaraijima village, William Chambliss (1965:94) found that the total tax burden of the marginal peasants (who represented twenty-three of the fifty households in his sample) had increased to seven times the pre-Restoration amount, whereas the taxes of the wealthier peasants had decreased by two thirds. Increases in local taxes contributed to this burden: between 1880 and 1883, prefectural land taxes rose by thirty-nine percent and town and village taxes rose by nineteen percent (Bowen, 1980:95). The government's deflationary policy of 1881, which substantially increased the real value of taxes (peasants were obliged to sell forty-two percent more of their crops in 1885 than in 1881 to pay their land taxes), further exacerbated an already grim situation (Bowen, 1980:95). Thomas C. Smith (1955:83) estimates that "something in the order of eleven percent of all peasant proprietors were dispossessed for non-payment of taxes between 1883 and 1890." Accordingly, the amount of land under tenant cultivation increased from twenty-nine percent in 1872 to over forty percent in 1888 (Bowen, 1980:92). The dramatic increases in mortgages, compulsory sales, and bankruptcies in the 1880s and 1890s further testify to "the whirlwind speed of peasant expropriation during this period" (Norman, 1940:145).

As one would expect, this process of expropriation had a profound effect on labor market conditions, contributing to the increase in the proportion of the total labor force employed in non-agricultural labor from less than ten percent in 1872 to twenty-one percent in 1886 (Ohkawa and Rosovsky, 1965:90). Unfortunately, Japan's fledgling industrial sector, although growing rapidly, was unable to absorb such a large number of people, a situation which did not change until after the Sino-Japanese War. As a result, the intervening decades found the dispossessed peasantry caught in a desperate limbo between a shrinking agricultural sector and meager industrial opportunities (Norman, 1940:159-160). Even the traditional domestic industries such as cotton yarn and fabric production, rape seed oil manufacture, sugar cultivation, and paper making had, by the 1870s, been replaced by cheap foreign imports or large-scale mechanization. The dispossessed peasantry was thus forced into the lowest strata of unskilled labor, their lives, like Deguchi Nao's, "marked by the irregularity and insecurity of work or, when employed, by extremely long hours and low wages" (Norman, 1940:158). Some found work as day laborers, rickshaw drivers, longshoremen, or construction workers for the railroads. Others, like Nao and her daughter Hisa, peddled food or rags, or opened wayside refreshment stands. The more "fortunate" ones, usually women, found employment on a temporary or seasonal basis in the textile factories.

The dependence on textile production as a source of supplementary income had a long history in Japan. Prior to the Meiji Restoration in 1868, sericulture, spinning, and weaving were done largely by women in their homes. By the 1870s, however, textile production had moved out of the home and into the factory. In an effort to reduce foreign imports of textiles (which comprised one-half of Japan's imports from 1868 to 1882), the government actively encouraged the modernization and expansion of the textile industry. As a result, the textile industry grew rapidly, playing an important, if transitional, role in Japan's industrialization. By 1880, silk accounted for forty-three percent of all exports, providing much of the capital necessary for the later development of heavy industry (Fairbank, et al., 1965:249).

Until the late 1880s, seventy percent of this silk was hand-reeled by female laborers. Working conditions in these factories (as well as living conditions in the dormitories where many workers were housed) were miserable. The women worked fifteen hours a day at machines which were run at very high speeds. They were subjected to harsh disciplinary measures and often suffered from severe exhaustion and malnutrition. Their wages, moreover, were barely adequate to support a single adult (Taira, 1970:108). Yet, as we have seen, employment in these factories was an essential source of income for the dispossessed peasantry and urban poor. By 1892, however, increased mechanization (silk reeled by steam or water power produced a better quality silk and required only modest capital) had completely eliminated the hand-reeling method (Yasumaru, 1977:60) and the poor accordingly lost one of their most important sources of supplementary income.

One effect, therefore, of the economic depression triggered by government reforms and industrialization in the first three decades of the Meiji period was the creation of a semi-employed, impoverished population in the cities and villages. Cut off from former modes of employment in agriculture and domestic industry, the marginal peasant was left with few alternative means of support. The newspapers of 1884 reported that the number of paupers had greatly increased in many districts and that some were so desperate "they might resort to violence" (Bowen, 1980:96). A merchant speaking at a cotton and silk producers convention in 1885 assessed the situation as follows:

> [The depression] has not hurt the nobility, the bureaucrats, the scholars, the priests, or the industrialists. Those who are suffering most are the farmers. Their wives scream they are cold because they have no warm

> clothing. Their children yell they are hungry because
> they have no rice to eat. Such is the terrible lot of the
> farmers. They have to suffer the laws and the courts
> because of creditors. They have to sell their homes and
> land, that which has been the source of their livelihood
> and the livelihood of their ancestors... Farmers cannot
> afford to buy manufactured products, either -- they who
> should be our best customers (quoted in Bowen, 1980:99).

For the increasing number of people caught in this desperate economic plight, a commitment to the *tsūzoku dōtoku* came to serve less as a force of social integration than as a source of dissatisfaction with, and alienation from, the dominant sociopolitical order.

The prosperity and perpetuation of the *ie*, which adherence to the moral tenets of the *tsūzoku dōtoku* was supposed to guarantee, depended as much on an economic system supportive of the small producer and wage earner as on the diligence and frugality of all household members (Yasumaru, 1977:71-72). As we have seen, however, in the closing decades of the nineteenth century the Japanese government and economy, far from insuring the security of the small producer, actually threatened it. Against such great political and economic odds, the efforts of the marginal peasant to achieve even a small measure of financial security (let alone prosperity) were continually thwarted. Many, like Nao, were reduced to a day-to-day, subsistence level existence. Given the scarcity of employment opportunities, the low wages for what little work was available and the heavy tax burdens, marginal peasants were rarely able to improve their lot in life, no matter how patiently and diligently they and their families worked. Even the credit system established by the government was weighted against them. Legislation in 1880 prohibited the deferred payment of taxes and earlier laws actually encouraged usury:

> The Interest Limitation Law of September 11, 1877, set
> the legal maximum interest chargeable for private loans of
> under one hundred yen -- an amount applicable to the vast
> majority of farmers seeking credit -- at twenty percent per
> annum. Article Two of the same law, however, forbade
> litigation in cases where people exceeded the limits,
> thereby giving the creditor the right to exploit with
> impunity tight market conditions (Bowen, 1980:97-98).

A consideration of Nao's life and thought in this larger historical context allows us to firmly establish her identification with the collective experience and consciousness which we have just described as characteristic of the marginal peasant oppressed by the economic policies of the Meiji state. We know from Nao's own writings that she shared in the economic plight and world view of this particular social group. Nao spent most of her life in abject poverty and her desperate circumstances were aggravated rather than alleviated by Meiji reforms and industrialization. The values and expectations implicit in the *tsūzoku dōtoku* were, moreover, an integral part of her character and outlook on life. Like that of other marginal peasants, Nao's unceasing struggle to better her lot proved futile in a socioeconomic system and political climate inimical to the security of the propertyless poor.

Nao's parents fell into destitution from a position of relative wealth when she was still a child and, although the Deguchis were quite well off at the time of their marriage, their financial situation followed a similar pattern of decline. Carpentry, compared to many other means of earning a living, was a steady and potentially lucrative occupation, but Nao's husband was not as successful as he might have been. It was thus necessary for Nao to supplement the family income with first a small restaurant and later her *manjū* business. In spite of Nao's efforts, however, the Deguchis eventually lost all of their property and in 1884, overwhelmed by extremely high taxes and interest rates, were forced into bankruptcy. When Masagorō's accident in the following year completely incapacitated him, Nao had no alternative but to take up rag collecting in order to support her family. With her husband's death in 1887, Nao finally sank to the lowest rung of the socioeconomic ladder.

In the Ayabe records of 1894, there is a separate category for households with an annual income of fifteen yen or less -- at that time, fifteen yen was the price of two *koku* of rice. Of the thirty-three families included in this category, nine earned their livelihood by collecting and selling rags and thirteen were either headed by widows or in similarly difficult circumstances (Yasumaru, 1977:46). Rag collecting was thus only one small step above begging. To supplement these meager earnings, Nao also worked on a seasonal basis in local silk reeling factories. Here, too, however, she suffered the same fate as other marginal peasants dependent on employment in the rapidly modernizing textile industry.

In the Tamba region where Nao lived, the cultivation and production of cotton and silk had been an important industry since the end of the Tokugawa period. Until the 1870s, spinning cotton thread was a popular home industry and silk was produced almost entirely by hand well into the 1880s. But after the introduction of steam-operated spinning and reeling machines in 1882 and the establishment of an organization in 1886 to facilitate the modernization and expansion of the silk industry in the districts around Kyoto, the textile industry, especially in the Ayabe area, swiftly mechanized. After 1887, hand reeling and spinning machines had become rare and Nao had to travel as far as Kameoka to find factory employment. By 1891, hand-operated machines had been completely eliminated. Yasumaru has suggested that this rather sudden loss of a source of income essential to the subsistence of many families in the region perhaps accounts in part for the unusually high number of cases of insanity (twenty-eight) recorded for 1891 in the district which included Ayabe (Yasumaru, 1977:58-60). It is suggestive to recall in this context that Nao's eldest daughter, Yone, went mad at the end of that same year and that Nao's first *kamigakari*, which she and others initially identified as madness, occurred very early in the following year.

All of the occupations that Nao engaged in were typical of the very poor who lacked both the skills and capital to do anything else. Members of her immediate family as well as many of her neighbors also depended for their subsistence on such low-paying, insecure occupations. Nao's father had peddled sake and her mother had spun cotton thread in her home. Nao's daughter, Hisa, married a rickshaw driver and operated a small, wayside restaurant. Nao's neighborhood of Motomiyamura was, moreover, the home of many of Ayabe's poor. Her neighbors included small farmers, itinerant merchants, day laborers, artisans such as carpenters and plasterers, and former samurai families forced into destitution after the cancellation of their stipends (Yasumaru, 1977:60-61). Sumi's memoirs provide further information about "the many unhappy people" who lived in Motomiyamura in the 1880s and 1890s: from a total of thirty-one households, there were thirteen people who were either in prison or who had prison records, some of them thieves and murderers; thirteen people who suffered from a physical handicap such as blindness or the loss of one arm; and five incidents of suicide (Yasumaru, 1977:61). Nao was thus speaking from personal experience when she wrote in 1903 that "there are many people at the bottom of Japanese society who, after working hard all day, still have nothing to eat. Nevertheless, government administrators at the top of society do not understand that there is such extreme suffering" (quoted in Yasumaru, 1977:194).

Nao shared not only the experience of hardship and suffering with the marginal peasant, but a consciousness grounded in the *tsūzoku dōtoku* as well. She had learned this conventional morality as a child and her commitment to it was further reinforced by her years of employment in the large merchant households of Fukuchiyama. Shingaku theories which, as we noted earlier, were an important source of the *tsūzoku dōtoku*, were very popular among Fukuchiyama merchants (Yasumaru, 1977:24). The award Nao received for her filial piety, honesty, and diligence was a public acknowledgement of her conformity to conventional moral standards and a powerful confirmation of her expectation that such conformity was a guarantee of social respect. As an adult, Nao's strict adherence to this ethical code gave her a sense of personal dignity and pride so strong that not even total destitution could undermine it.

The fact that Nao shared in a popular consciousness informed by the *tsūzoku dōtoku* is further confirmed by her commitment to one of its central values -- the perpetuation of the *ie*. Once Nao had resigned herself to adoption and marriage into the Deguchi family, she devoted herself to its maintenance and perpetuation. As we have seen, however, her unflagging efforts in this direction were constantly frustrated: first by her husband's financial blunders and general indolence and later by bankruptcy and the death of her most responsible son. By the 1890s, Nao had probably begun to fear, as had her aunt before her, that the Deguchi family line would surely expire. How could an impoverished widow with only two young daughters left at home possibly insure the future prosperity of her family? In this respect, it is interesting to view Nao's efforts to establish Ōmotokyō following her *kamigakari* in 1892 as, in part, efforts to perpetuate the Deguchi *ie*, for Ōmotokyō was (and still is today) in many ways a successful "family enterprise." She eventually adopted her son-in-law and co-founder, Onisaburō, so that his children would be Deguchis not only through their mother, Sumi, but in name also. The common practice of adopting male heirs to continue the family line was well-known to Nao: her husband, Masagorō, represented the third generation of adopted male heirs in the Deguchi family. This practice was later institutionalized in Ōmotokyō, for the highest position of spiritual leadership in the organization is reserved for direct female descendants of Nao whose husbands are adopted into the Deguchi family.

For Nao, therefore, and for others like her, the implicit promise of the *tsūzoku dōtoku* that one's diligent labor and righteous behavior would be justly rewarded was broken by the forces of political and economic change. Experience had come to contradict rather than validate the life cycle projected by the conventional moral paradigm. The general perception of this contradiction did not necessarily lead, however, to a rejection of the assumptions and expectations implicit in the *tsūzoku dōtoku*, but rather to a loud and often active opposition to those government reforms which, by robbing many peasants of their autonomy and livelihood, had generated the contradiction. This bitter indictment drew much of its legitimacy, moreover, from those same assumptions and expectations which we have identified with the *tsūzoku dōtoku*. In the consciousness of those excluded from Meiji progress, the role of the *tsūzoku dōtoku* was thus transformed from a source of integration into the prevailing social system to a reference point for a radical critique of the established order. Let us now turn to a consideration of Nao's place as the founder of a new religion in this pattern of popular protest and social criticism.

Folk Religion and Popular Protest: The Establishment of a Millenarian Cult

The first three decades of the Meiji period were marked by a high incidence of peasant uprisings which were either explicitly anti-government or had strong anti-government undertones. One of the earliest Meiji rebellions occurred in Ayabe in 1873 when over two thousand peasants marched on the local government office to protest high taxes, universal military conscription, and the printing of bank securities and bonds. They also protested other recently enacted policies such as the prohibition of open pastures for the free grazing of livestock and the transfer of public rice reserves from the village to the district administrative level. After confronting the government officials with their demands, most of the rebels returned home. The incident so alarmed the authorities, however, that they arrested twenty-two people and alerted a nearby encampment of government troops in case further riots occurred (Yasumaru, 1977:64).

In contrast to such early Meiji rebellions, later uprisings were specifically aimed at the wealthy landlords and merchants who, having clearly benefitted from Meiji reforms, were seen as willing accomplices in the government's relentless exploitation and oppression of the small producer (Bowen, 1980:92, 307). Many of these rebels invoked the symbols and slogans of the newly formed Movement for Freedom and Popular Rights (Jiyū Minken Undō) to give legitimacy and coherence to their anti-government activities. They demanded an economic system more sympathetic to the small producer and a representative form of government (Bowen, 1980:304). In his detailed study of these rebellions, Roger W. Bowen argues that they manifested the farmer's consciousness of possessing rights vis-à-vis the authorities (1980:115-116). Meiji farmers, according to Bowen, realized that the interests being served by the present government conflicted with their own. Moreover, they understood that in order to protect and further their own interests they must control the state or at least modify its authority to arbitrarily exploit them (1980:307). Bowen concludes, therefore, that Meiji rebellions represented not merely peasant discontent, but a fundamental questioning of the legitimacy of the established sociopolitical order (1980:307).

Although Nao, following her *kamigakari*, came to share the Meiji rebels' bitter opposition to the government, she never took part in a peasant uprising or condoned the violent methods and liberal ideologies employed by the participants. A clue to this apparent inconsistency lies in Bowen's assessment of the socioeconomic status of the rebels who supported the Jiyū Minken Undō. He found that the participants in such uprisings were primarily middle level farmers -- a rural bourgeoisie, as it were (1980:173). Yasumaru Yoshio likewise points out that the Ayabe branch of the Jiyūtō was dominated by landlords and budding rural capitalists (1977:66). Thus, the Movement for Freedom and Popular Rights, like the Meiji state, in no way represented the interests of people like Nao who owned no property and were dependent for their subsistence on insecure and seasonal forms of wage labor. Yasumaru argues that Nao, realizing this, harbored no illusions about the Jiyū Minken Undō (1977:67).

Nao's mode of resistance, her vision of the ideal society, and the interests she claimed to represent were thus substantially different from those of the Meiji rebels who claimed an ideological and often organizational affiliation with the Jiyūtō. To legitimize her social criticism and her call for a more equitable social order, Nao invoked not a liberal theory of natural human rights, but a folk religious theory of divine inspiration and authority (*kamigakari*) on the one hand and a popular ideal of human righteousness, community, and social justice (the *tsūzoku dōtoku*) on the other.

Looking at Japanese society from the perspective of this moral paradigm, Nao saw a world in which "the strong prey upon the weak" (quoted in Hino 1974:1) and "people are thrown down and trampled like the cast off heads of rice" (quoted in Yasumaru, 1977:207). She saw a world in which "human selfishness and avarice know no bounds" (quoted in Hino, 1974:21), and human compassion and generosity were no longer valued: "A person could fall into ruin and drop dead and no one would care, for [people today] are concerned only with themselves" (quoted in Yasumaru, 1977:36). She saw a world in which money and power, not moral virtue, were the measure of an individual's worth. In Nao's view, it was an evil world indeed where those who were selfish and greedy prospered while those who were righteous and diligent suffered.

Nao believed that the primary instigators and perpetuators of this evil were the government and the Emperor. She accused the Emperor of having a "foreign spirit" and predicted the destruction of his government. In the divine realm that Ushitora-no-Konjin would establish, there would be no artificial governments, nations, or kings. High and low would be equal, the Emperor would be like an ordinary person, and all the people of the world would be united under the divine rule of Ushitora-no-Konjin (Yasumaru, 1977:200). In accordance with this rejection of the legitimacy and authority of the Meiji state, Nao was also very critical of the nationalistic doctrines being taught in the public schools and propagated through State Shinto. Denouncing the Emperor cult as a lie, she insisted that Amaterasu no longer resided at Ise because it had become such an evil place and that the Emperor was actually a "four-legged guardian deity." The world, in her view, was being controlled by evil, not good, *kami* (Yasumaru, 1977:144-145).

It is Nao's description of the divine realm Ushitora-no-Konjin would create on earth which constitutes her strongest condemnation of the Meiji government and sociocultural order, for Nao's vision of the ideal society was radically different from that envisioned for Japan by its ruling and economic elite. In Nao's ideal world, everyone would live in harmony and equality under the just and compassionate rule of Ushitora-no-Konjin and in pious dependence on the generosity of Heaven and Nature. There would be no wars, poverty, sickness, or suffering and everyone would lead long, happy, comfortable lives. It would, however, be a simple, frugal society rather than one of wealth and luxury. People would be self-supporting and cooperate rather than compete with one another. They would grow their own food and rely on natural products for all necessities like clothing and housing. There would be no money. No one would eat meat (only fish, grains, fruit, and vegetables) and there would be no wastefulness. There would be no silk, no tobacco, no western style clothes or shoes, no fancy sweets or cakes, and no gambling. All celebrations would be very simple. There would be no need for learning or scholarship because everything would be clear and easily understood by everyone. Laws (and the policemen who enforced them) would also be unnecessary for all human beings would be pure in spirit, diligent in their labor, honest, and sincere (Yasumaru, 1977:203-207).

Nao's vision of an earthly paradise is clearly a religious projection of the values and way of life ideally prescribed by the *tsūzoku dōtoku*. It represents, moreover, a complete rejection of the capitalistic model of society being pursued by the Meiji state through its policies of industrialization and westernization. In this respect, it is, as Yasumaru Yoshio has argued, "a vivid crystallization" of an ideal of human community and morality implicit in the collective consciousness of the Japanese folk -- a utopian vision based on their concerns and aspirations rather than those of the ruling elite (1977:208-209). If we may define revolutionary thinking as a means whereby the oppressed break out of the system in which they are dominated, then Nao's vision of reality, both present and future, must be seen as revolutionary. By constructing a world view representative of the experience and consciousness (the interests) of those oppressed by Meiji policies, Nao transformed the Japanese folk from objects in a reality created by the state to subjects acting in terms of their own definition of reality, their own values and expectations. In other words, Nao transformed those who had heretofore seen themselves as helpless victims of social forces beyond their control into social reformers with the power and knowledge to remake the world according to a design of their own creation. Nao wrote in the *Ofudesaki* that:

> The reconstruction of this world will not be accomplished through learning, cleverness, wisdom, money, or laws. Furthermore, neither military force, nor the present system of government, nor what is being taught in the schools will help bring it about (quoted in Yasumaru, 1977:70).

Rather, in Nao's view, social transformation would be brought about through the divine power of Ushitora-no-Konjin which was realized in the daily efforts of ordinary men and women to purify their spirits and reform their lives in accordance with his will. It is this revolutionary character of Nao's world view that Yasumaru Yoshio wished to emphasize when he described her *Ofudesaki* as "a fundamental protest against cruelty and a cry for emancipation" (1977:7).

The fact that Nao's protest was decidedly religious in form and content does not mean, therefore, that it was not political. We may extend Bowen's insistence that "rebels do not have to explicitly raise questions about the structure and control of government in order to qualify as political actors" (1980:307) to Nao as well, for her thought and action, like that of the rebels, clearly challenged the legitimacy of established political authority. It could even be argued that Nao's revolutionary vision was far more radical than that of the Jiyūtō rebels: rather than demanding a determining role in the prevailing power structure, she insisted on its complete destruction. This revolutionary vision of the ideal society was shared, moreover, by many other nineteenth century religious movements which, like Ōmotokyō, were rooted in the consciousness and experience of the Japanese folk (Yasumaru, 1977:208). Recognizing these movements as a threat to their political and ideological hegemony, the Meiji government instituted tight controls over them. Groups lacking government authorization were not permitted to hold public meetings and religious leaders whose teachings did not conform with those of State Shinto were subjected to official persecution and suppression (Kitagawa, 1966:221). In order to survive, most of these groups were forced to reconcile their doctrines with the religious and political ideology of State Shinto. This constant threat of government suppression was a determining factor in the establishment of Ōmotokyō and the development of its doctrine, as well as a primary source of tension between Nao and her co-founder, Onisaburō.

Any effort to understand the historical significance of the new religions must, therefore, take into account their essentially political character. Among the few social movements which represented the aspirations of the lower classes, these religious associations were open to marginal peasants who lacked the influence, organization, and education to otherwise articulate their opposition to the state and work for change. At the end of the Tokugawa period and into the early Meiji period, vast numbers of the rural and urban poor participated in pilgrimages to temples and shrines (primarily Ise Jingū) called *okage mairi* and *eejanaika*.[18] Those involved in these spontaneous religious movements demanded emancipation from economic oppression and called for broad social reform (Oguchi and Takagi, 1956:317). It soon became apparent, however, that the Meiji Restoration of 1868 had failed to create the more equitable social order they had hoped it would. Although these particular forms of religious resistance did not occur after the first years of the Meiji period, the rural and urban poor who had participated in the *okage mairi* and *eejanaika* continued to seek a voice for their views and a resolution of their socioeconomic problems in other folk religious practices and movements which expressed their hope for *yonaoshi* or "world renewal."

These Meiji religious movements included devotional associations (*kō*) that sponsored pilgrimages to sacred places like Mt. Fuji and Mt. Ontake, and lay organizations like Tenrikyō and Konkōkyō which experienced their most rapid growth in the last decades of the nineteenth century. Like the popular Tokugawa *kō* with which they hold much in common, these movements represented a new form of social organization

---

[18] *Okage mairi* means literally "worship to return divine favor." "*Eejanaika*" means "anything goes" or "why not, it's okay."

which transcended established institutional structures and aimed for the creation of new forms of association based on a shared belief in world renewal and the salvation of the individual. They projected, moreover, a new vision of society based on social equality and mutual economic assistance rather than hierarchy and competition (Murakami, 1971:569). In particular, the founder of Tenrikyō, Nakayama Miki, took an explicitly anti-government stance and was sharply critical of the wealthy, ruling classes. Believing that the gods were on the side of the ruled rather than the rulers, she consciously cast herself as a representative of the oppressed lower classes (Oguchi and Takagi, 1956:327-334).

Nao was not only aware of these religious movements, but right from the beginning explicitly acknowledged her place in this religious tradition of protest and identified her mission as a critical contribution to the ongoing effort to achieve social reform and world renewal. In her first entry in the *Ofudesaki* (dated January, 1892), Nao wrote:

> First came Tenri, Konkō, Kurozumi, and Myōrei, but now, finally, Ushitora-no-Konjin has revealed (his plan) to bring about the reconstruction of the world. Although these other religions understand something about the reformation of the world, they do not know how to carry it out (quoted in Kozawa, 1973:158).

In spite of her later criticism of Tenrikyō and Konkōkyō, Nao initially sought affiliation with both because she was convinced that the similarities between her revelations and these movements were as important as the differences. Exhibiting a strong historical consciousness of her own religious role, Nao believed that her *kamigakari* qualified her to build upon the foundation laid by these earlier movements. Nao's claim to uniqueness and superiority as regards her religious message must thus be viewed in the context of this sense of historical continuity which pervades her thought.

During the two years immediately following her *kamigakari*, Nao was able to gather a number of followers through her faith healing practices. Her rag collecting provided her with ample opportunities to tell others about her *kami* and use his power to heal the sick. She grew increasingly frustrated, however, by her failure to establish an organized cult focused on Ushitora-no-Konjin and her revelations of his will. In her *Ofudesaki*, she insisted again and again that Ushitora-no-Konjin was not merely a healer of the sick, but a *kami* who corrected spirits and had a plan to reconstruct the world. Finally, in the spring of 1894, Nao visited the

Kameoka branch of Konkōkyō in the hope that they would help her fulfill her mission of world salvation and renewal.

The Konkō leaders in Kameoka had heard of Nao and knew that she had a reputation as a powerful faith healer, but they were not interested in her *Ofudesaki* and told her to return to Ayabe. Undaunted, Nao instead traveled on to Kyoto and visited the Tenrikyō headquarters located there. The Tenri leaders looked at her *Ofudesaki*, but insisted that it contained nothing that Nakayama Miki had not already said. Infuriated by this rejection, Nao experienced a severe attack of *kamigakari*. Unfortunately, this only served to further convince the Tenri leaders that she was suffering from fox possession and they, too, sent her away (Yasumaru, 1977:112). Angry and discouraged, Nao returned to Ayabe and her rag collecting and faith healing.

Several months later, however, she once again visited the Konkō branch in Kameoka. This time she requested the establishment of a new Konkōkyō church in Ayabe. She and her followers wanted a place where they could all worship Ushitora-no-Konjin together. The Konkō leaders were delighted and immediately dispatched one of their teachers, Okumura Sadajirō, to organize the new church. Ignoring Nao's radical revelations and social criticism, they decided to exploit her powers of faith healing to attract new members and spread their own teachings, a proselytization technique often employed by the more established new religions (Yasumaru, 1977:115). Nao, however, mistakenly interpreted their interest as an affirmation of the power of her *kami* and the truth of his revelations. Unlike the Konkō leaders, she believed that her Ushitora-no-Konjin was the same *kami* who had originally possessed Konkō's recently deceased founder, Kawate Bunjirō, and that her mission was thus a continuation of his.

In Ayabe, Okumura rented a six-mat room and opened the new Konkōkyō *hiromae* or church. Nao lived there with him and, in addition to her religious duties, served as his housekeeper. Her *Ofudesaki* was placed on the altar as the *shintai*[19] for Ushitora-no-Konjin and he was worshipped along with the *kami* of Konkōkyō, Tenchi Kane no Kami. Regular worship services were held three times a month. The group grew rapidly and had to keep moving to larger quarters. By the end of that same year, there were 360 members (Yasumaru, 1977:117).

---

[19] *Shintai* is the Shinto term for an object of worship which symbolizes a particular deity or in which the spirit of a deity is believed to reside.

In spite of this rapid increase in membership, Nao grew more and more dissatisfied with Okumura. She had hoped that he would clarify the meaning of her *kamigakari* and explain her *Ofudesaki* to others. Okumura, however, showed no interest in the *Ofudesaki* and ignored Nao's demands that he acknowledge the absolute authority of her *kami* (Yasumaru, 1977:118). Frustrated and angry, Nao left Ayabe in the spring of 1895 and stayed with relatives in Yagi and Fukuchiyama where she worked in silk reeling factories and pursued her faith healing activities. The Tenri church in Yagi asked her to join them, but she refused and finally returned to Ayabe early in 1896 (Yasumaru, 1977:120).

Shortly after her return, Okumura held a great festival at the Ayabe *hiromae*. People from as far away as Osaka and Kyoto attended. Convinced that Konkōkyō's success in Ayabe was the result of his own efforts, Okumura hid the *Ofudesaki* so that no one would discover the important role played by Nao and her *kami*. His plan backfired: when Nao realized what he had done, she experienced a wild state of *kamigakari* and severly criticized Okumura in front of all his guests. Following this incident, she once again left Ayabe and stayed away for several months. During her absence, most members stopped attending Konkōkyō services. Completely humiliated, Okumura fled and was never heard from again (Yasumaru, 1977:121).

When Nao heard that Okumura had disappeared, she returned to Ayabe and she and her followers once again gathered at the former Konkō *hiromae*. The Konkō leaders in Kameoka did not want to lose this newly opened territory, however, and later that year sent another teacher, Adachi Sadanobu, to take charge of the group. Unfortunately, Adachi proved to be as uninterested in the *Ofudesaki* as his predecessor had been. In 1897, Nao moved to a different house in Ayabe and held worship services there exclusively for Ushitora-no-Konjin. Passages in the *Ofudesaki* written during this period read like "a declaration of independence from Konkōkyō" (Yasumaru, 1977:123).

Nao's irreconcilable conflicts with Okumura and Adachi stemmed from their stubborn refusal both to acknowledge the supreme authority of the *kami* who had possessed her and clarify the meaning of his revelations which she recorded almost daily in her *Ofudesaki*; from their refusal, in other words, to acknowledge Nao's vision of reality. Assuming that they shared similar religious goals, Nao joined Konkōkyō with the expectation that its teachers would prove the power of her *kami* and the truth of his revelations. She hoped, moreover, that they would help her to formulate a cohesive doctrine based on these revelations (Yasumaru, 1977:118).

However, Adachi and Okumura did not share either Nao's assumptions or goals. Although Ushitora-no-Konjin was the *kami* to first possess Konkōkyō's founder, in the development of Konkō doctrine his identity was gradually transformed into the supreme creator and savior deity of the universe, Tenchi Kane no Kami (Schneider, 1962:117-118). Okumura and Adachi could not believe that such a great *kami* would choose a poor, uneducated woman like Nao as his medium and thus viewed her as just another faith healer whose power derived from some other less important deity. Her teachings were, moreover, radically different from their own.

According to the *Ofudesaki*, the world was a completely evil place which must be destroyed so that a new divine realm could be established. Nao's harsh social criticism, her eschatological predictions, and her utopian vision of an earthly paradise contrasted sharply with Konkō doctrine which instead emphasized the renewal of the individual's bond with *kami* through a ritualized mode of spiritual mediation called *otoritsugi*. Such divine communion and renewal were believed to guarantee not only the individual's ultimate salvation, but his or her health and prosperity in the present as well. Given their commitment to Konkō doctrines, it is not surprising, therefore, that Okumura and Adachi showed little interest in the *Ofudesaki* and viewed Nao's "divine revelations" as the meaningless rantings of an old woman. They were far more concerned with spreading their own teachings and increasing the membership of Konkōkyō than with Nao's *kami* or revelations. The national leaders of Konkōkyō would not have permitted them to support Nao's criticism of the Meiji government and State Shinto anyway, for, in order to acquire official status as an independent religious organization, they had found it necessary to conform to national educational policies and State Shinto doctrines.[20] Having been co-opted by the State in this fashion, the interests of the Konkōkyō leaders were antagonistic to rather than coincident with Nao's own concerns and religious aspirations. In this respect, Nao's separation from Adachi in 1897 was perhaps motivated by her gradual realization that the Konkō leaders had merely been exploiting her for their own purposes (Yasumaru, 1977:125).

Although Nao and her followers were pleased with this new independent arrangement, a total break with Konkōkyō would have incurred police intervention. In order to continue meeting together, therefore, Nao's group was forced to maintain a nominal affiliation with the officially recognized Konkō church. Moreover, Nao had still not resolved her major

---

[20] In 1882, Konkōkyō was authorized as one of the thirteen Shinto sects. Not until 1900 was it granted the official status of an independent religion.

problem. Although the basic elements of her religious view -- that Ushitora-no-Konjin would protect those who obeyed him and after destroying the present evil world create a new divine realm on earth -- were clear enough to Nao and her followers, she was still unable to structure her revelations into a broad, coherent doctrine of universal salvation and establish rituals which would help Ushitora-no-Konjin realize his plan of world reconstruction. Entries in the *Ofudesaki* recorded during this period express Nao's growing impatience to begin her mission of world renewal and her irritation that she was unable to do this herself (Yasumaru, 1977:126). She continued to hope that someone able to determine and verify (*miwakeru*) the origin, nature, and supreme power of Ushitora-no-Konjin would soon appear and help her to make his will known to the world.[21]

This phase of organizational and doctrinal limbo lasted until the spring of 1899 when Ueda Kisaburō (who later took the name of Deguchi Onisaburō) joined Nao in Ayabe. Together they founded the Kimmei Reigaku Society with Nao as the group's spiritual leader and Onisaburō as its president. Onisaburō had first heard of Nao from her daughter, Hisa, while traveling through Yagi the previous year. Although he visited Nao a few months later and was extremely interested in her *Ofudesaki*, he stayed only long enough to convince Nao that he would be able to help her (Yasumaru, 1977:156-157). In the spring of 1899, Nao sent one of her followers to Sonobe where Onisaburō lived to request his cooperation in the establishment of an independent religious organization. He agreed and returned to Ayabe.

Onisaburō was born in 1871 to a poor family of dairy farmers in Anao, a small village about thirty-seven miles southeast of Ayabe. Well educated for a man of his social status, Onisaburō pursued a number of different occupations, but none satisfied him. In February, 1898, at the age of twenty-seven, he went to a mountain near his home for a week of ascetic exercises. During his lonely vigil on the mountain, he claimed to have traveled through the spirit world.[22] This experience was the beginning of

---

[21] This is written in the *Ofudesaki* as: *"kai o yo ni dasu"* and *"kami o hyō e dasu."* According to Ōmoto doctrine, the true nature of Ushitora-no-Konjin had been hidden from the world until Nao's *kamigakari*. It was thus Nao's mission to make everyone aware of his absolute authority and intention to reconstruct the world (Yasumaru, 1977:161-162).

[22] For a more detailed account in English of Onisaburō's experiences on Mt. Takakuma and his travels through the spirit world, see Blacker, 1971:202-207. Onisaburō published a description of this initiatory experience in 1921. It constitutes the first eleven volumes of his *Reikai monogatari*, one of the sacred texts of Ōmotokyō.

Onisaburō's career as a religious specialist. Returning to Anao, he quickly developed a reputation as a successful faith healer and later that year was invited to visit the headquarters of the Inari-kō school of Shinto in Shizuoka where he studied with the school's head, Nagasawa Katsutoshi (Yasumaru, 1977:158-159).

Nagasawa was a disciple of Honda Chikaatsu, a Kokugaku scholar who was instrumental in introducing esoteric practices into Shinto after it was nationalized by the Meiji government. One such practice was a method of spirit possession and divination called *chinkonkishin* in which one individual, the *kannushi* (often a woman) blows on a stone to induce a state of *kamigakari* while her male partner, the *saniwa*, determines the identity of the possessing spirit. As a form of meditation and exorcism, *chinkonkishin* enabled its practitioners to purify their souls and achieve communion with the divine. As a means of communication with the spirit world, however, it also empowered its proponents, like Nagasawa, to attribute power and rank to otherwise unknown deities and thus incorporate popular beliefs into State Shinto (Yasumaru, 1977:161).

After studying with Nagasawa, Onisaburō returned to Anao and established an organization based on the practice of *chinkonkishin*. He spent most of his time, however, wandering from village to village in the area around Anao, spreading his teachings and offering his services as a *saniwa*. It was in this role of itinerant faith healer, exorcist, and diviner of spirits that Onisaburō first met Nao. Realizing the complementarity of their religious skills, they decided that together they would be better able to achieve their religious aspirations.

For most of the first year of their long and otherwise stormy association, Nao was completely satisfied with Onisaburō. His connections with Inari-kō finally enabled her to establish an officially recognized organization independent of Konkōkyō. Moreover, the young *saniwa* was able to identify Nao's *kami* as the Shinto deity Kunitakehiko-no-mikoto and verify his supreme power. Under this new name, Ushitora-no-Konjin was made the central deity of the organization and worshipped exclusively by its members. Nao was overjoyed -- at last, the truth about Ushitora-no-Konjin had been demonstrated and a movement dedicated to informing others of his plan to reconstruct the world had been initiated. On January 1, 1900, Nao publicly indicated her approval of Onisaburō and firmly established his position in the group as second in command by allowing him to marry her daughter and proclaimed successor, Sumi.

Nao's initial pleasure with Onisaburō and the Kimmei Reigaku Society soon gave way, however, to increasing dissatisfaction with the group's espousal of State Shinto doctrines and involvement in the practice of *chinkonkishin*. Although Onisaburō claimed that the group must give evidence of adherence to the tenets of State Shinto in order to continue its activities without police intervention, Nao viewed such compromises, for whatever reason they were made, as a betrayal of Ushitora-no-Konjin's wishes. Despite the group's affiliation with Inari-kō, which supported State Shinto, Nao continued to criticize the Meiji government, its religious ideologies, and the Emperor. This issue was a constant source of conflict between Nao and Onisaburō, but the growing popularity of *chinkonkishin* among members of the group was even more disturbing to her than Onisaburō's efforts to appease the government authorities.

Following its establishment in the spring of 1899, the group had grown rapidly. Even Adachi left Konkōkyō and joined the Kimmei Reigaku Society (Yasumaru, 1977:165). To Nao's dismay, however, the primary reason for this increase in membership was the practice of *chinkonkishin*. Although spontaneous *kamigakari* was a commonly acknowledged phenomenon, a method of artificially induced *kamigakari* which enabled anyone to experience spirit possession was unusual. Thus, many people joined the group in order to practice *chinkonkishin* under Onisaburō's guidance. *Chinkonkishin* sessions were held on a regular group basis with as many as twenty people participating. Entering wild states of spirit possession, the participants would claim clairvoyant powers and predict the course of local and world events (Yasumaru, 1977:168). Not surprisingly, Nao became more and more adamant in her opposition to this practice. It belittled her own experience of *kamigakari* and threatened to undermine the authority of her *Ofudesaki*. It was, moreover, a form of self-indulgence which distracted the group from its primary purpose -- to clarify the teachings of Ushitora-no-Konjin and inform others of his plan to reconstruct the world.[23] In her *Ofudesaki*, Nao asserted the authority of her own

---

[23] In spite of Nao's adamant opposition, *chinkonkishin* continued to be practiced in Ōmotokyō well into the 1920s. Although many people were attracted to Ōmotokyō because of *chinkonkishin*, it also served as a source of conflict in the group. In 1923, while practicing *chinkonkishin*, Taniguchi Masaharu (1893-1985) experienced a series of revelations which inspired him to break with Ōmoto and establish his own religion, Seichō no Ie. Three years later, another close follower of Onisaburō, Okada Mokichi (1882-1955), was possessed by Kannon, the Buddhist goddess of mercy, while practicing *chinkonkishin*. On the basis of these revelations he, too, left Ōmoto and founded his own organization, Sekai Kyūsei Kyō. Nao's fears that this method of artificially induced *kamigakari* represented a potential threat to her own authority and mission were thus not unfounded. Onisaburō eventually dropped the practice of *chinkonkishin* and introduced a less radical method of achieving communion with

revelations and warned her followers of the negative consequences of an over-indulgence in *chinkonkishin* (translated below as "psychic studies"):

> If you are too engrossed in psychic studies, you will neglect the scriptures of Ushitora-no-Konjin and not act faithfully in compliance with his will. Thus, devote seventy percent [of your efforts] to his scriptures and only thirty percent to psychic studies... [Otherwise] you will cause people to misunderstand his Divine Plan and spoil the true teaching...[for] his will is always made known through the hand of Deguchi Nao... It is a bad habit for one to try to propagate the teachings by means of [*chinkonkishin*]... If you do not break this habit yourselves, you will be forced to open your eyes through more drastic means. Do you think you will be of any divine service while being made sport of by evil spirits?[24]

Unfortunately, Nao's warnings had little effect on either her followers or Onisaburō. Finding herself once again frustrated in her efforts to propagate the teachings of her *kami*, Nao finally took matters into her own hands in the spring of 1900. Up until that time, Nao had perceived her role as a passive one and had depended on others to explicate her doctrine. It was for this reason that Onisaburō's skills as a *saniwa* had initially seemed so well suited to her needs. The complementary roles of the two participants in *chinkonkishin* were directly analogous to the partnerships often established in Japanese folk religion between a male shaman (*yamabushi*) and a female medium. In both cases, the medium was considered a passive mouthpiece for communications from the spirit world, while the authority to determine the significance of these communications (by naming the possessing spirit and interpreting the meaning of its statements) was held by the shaman or *saniwa*. The medium's position was thus a subordinate one vis-à-vis her male partner.

As described in Chapter I, however, Nao's commitment to the divine revelations she made while in a state of trance forced her to break with the circumscribed role traditionally associated with female mediums.

---

the divine which did not involve *kamigakari*. Called *otoritsugi*, this method of meditation and spiritual purification is still practiced in Ōmotokyō today.

[24] Quoted in Hino, 1974:133-134. For the sake of clarity I have made some minor revisions in Hino's translation of this passage.

Far from being a passive mouthpiece for the will of the gods, Nao interpreted the significance of her revelations herself and acted in accordance with them. Her problem was that she lacked the verbal and organizational skills to communicate her religious views to others and establish an independent cult based on her own teachings. Nao's partnership with Onisaburō was thus a very ambivalent one which did not conform to the traditional pattern. Although she needed him to validate her experience of *kamigakari* and explain the meaning of her revelations to others, she was not willing to relinquish her authority when it came to interpreting her revelations. Nao expected Onisaburō to be a passive, but articulate, mouthpiece for *her* will. Unfortunately, Onisaburō disagreed with certain important aspects of Nao's teachings and refused to cooperate.

But this time, rather than running from the opposition as she had in the past run from Okumura and Adachi, Nao stood her ground and struggled to reassert the authority of her own religious views. Unable to convince her followers of the significance and urgency of her mission with verbal explanations and admonitions, Nao instead initiated a series of ritual activities called *shusshu* in which she put her teachings into practice. The term *shusshu* is peculiar to Ōmotokyō and is used only in reference to those ritual activities conducted between 1900 and 1905. It is composed of two characters: the first, *shutsu*, means here to go out, to expose, and to participate; the second, *shu*, means to cultivate, master and discipline oneself. As the first character implies, all of the *shusshu* involved pilgrimages to sacred sites determined by divine revelation. Although Nao was the principal actor in these pilgrimages, many of her followers also participated. Like the forms of popular pilgrimage which flourished during the Tokugawa period and continued well into the twentieth century, the *shusshu* were thus collective forms of ritualized activity. As such, they established a commonality of experience and purpose among Nao's followers and generated a powerful sense of group solidarity and identity.

The *shusshu* also constituted, however, a method of ritual expiation and a means for achieving salvation. This particular function of the *shusshu* is indicated by its second character, *shu*, which is also used in the popular term for ascetic practice or religious training and discipline, *shugyō*. Japanese religious specialists and laymen alike conducted *shugyō* not only as penance for past misdeeds, but also to enhance their spiritual purity and power, make contact with the spirit world, and increase their chances for salvation by reducing their bad karma. The performance of pilgrimages and certain purification rites such as *mizugori* (cold water ablutions) were common methods of *shugyō*, as were a variety of other religious practices and austerities including fasting and seclusion in desolate places. The *shusshu* thus provided Nao and her followers with opportunities to perform *shugyō*. The physical hardships they were made to endure, such as going for extended periods without food and sleep, walking great distances, and conducting frequent *mizugori*, were seen both as atonement for previous wrongdoings and as religious training and discipline.

In this respect, the *shusshu* enabled Nao to put into practice one of the principal tenets of her teachings: "Without going through difficulties, people are apt to be too proud; those who are to serve *kami* truly shall suffer considerable trials... Without pain, you cannot understand anything" (12/8/1901; Hino, 1974:86). Suffering, in Nao's view, was the primary source of humility, faith, and spiritual purity and goodness. She was convinced that the path to salvation was a difficult one. Moreover, only through suffering could one achieve a true understanding of the evil state of the world and its imminent reconstruction. Believing that it was her own profound suffering that had qualified her as Ushitora-no-Konjin's spokesperson, Nao insisted that only those who had endured grave hardships were able to serve her *kami* and receive his protection. Prior to the *shusshu*, Nao worried that her followers had not suffered enough, for their faith in Ushitora-no-Konjin's saving power was too easily shaken and they often failed to obey his teachings. As a form of *shugyō*, or ritualized suffering, the *shusshu* thus provided Nao's followers with an opportunity to reform their spirits, strengthen their faith, and insure their salvation through the performance of prescribed religious austerities.

The first two *shusshu* were conducted in the spring and summer of 1900. Early in June of that year, Nao received a revelation from Ushitora-no-Konjin ordering her to "go to Oshima for the second reconstruction of the world." Oshima is a small, deserted island in the Japan Sea about twenty miles from the coastal town of Maizuru (see Map 1, page 4). On the eighth of June, Nao, Onisaburō, Sumi, and two male followers left Ayabe and walked the fifteen miles to Maizuru. Arriving in the early evening, they went immediately to the local docks and asked two boatmen to row them out to the island. As the weather had become dark and stormy, the men at first refused. Impressed, however, by Nao's dignified and self-assured manner, they finally agreed when she promised that the wind and rain would stop as soon as they reached the entrance to Maizuru Bay. When they arrived at the entrance to the bay several hours later, just as Nao had predicted, the wind died down and the sky cleared. They reached Oshima early the next morning as the sun was rising above the horizon. After disembarking from their boat on the island's narrow beach, they performed cold water ablutions to purify themselves. Then they found the shrine where a spirit called Obitojima-myōjin was worshipped by the fishermen of the area. They cleaned the shrine, read the *Ōharae Norito* (an ancient Shinto liturgy of purification) and prayed to both Obitojima-Myōjin and Ushitora-no-Konjin. Following this brief ceremony, they rowed back to Maizuru and returned to Ayabe that evening (*Ōmoto nanajūnen-shi*, Vol.I, 1964:207-210).

A month later, Nao received another revelation, this one instructing her to go to Meshima, a small outcropping of rock two miles to the north of Oshima. On the eighth of July, Nao, together with Onisaburō, Sumi, and six followers, once again set out on foot for Maizuru. Requesting the services of the same boatmen as before, they rowed first to Oshima where they arrived at about eight the next morning. After reading the *Ōharae Norito* at the shrine and making offerings of fish, Nao, Onisaburō, Sumi, and two others went on to Meshima, leaving four men behind to clean the Oshima shrine precincts. Meshima has no beach, so it was difficult to find a place to moor the boat along its rocky cliffs. After circling the island, Nao finally ordered the boatmen to row up to a large, bell-shaped rock. Onisaburō jumped out and somehow managed to tie up the boat. After everyone had carefully disembarked and performed *mizugori*, they placed a small wooden shrine brought from Ayabe on a flat rock away from the sea. There they enshrined Ushitora-no-Konjin, presented offerings and prayed to him. Having successfully completed their mission, they rowed back to Maizuru where they had a commemorative photograph taken before returning to Ayabe (*Ōmoto nanajūnen-shi*, Vol. I, 1964:211-212).

As this account shows, the *shusshu* have much in common with other forms of Japanese religious practice and ritual. It also shows, however, that in creating the *shusshu* within the context of her own world view, Nao gave new meaning and purpose to these popular forms of pilgrimage, group worship, and ascetic practice. The primary meaning and purpose of the *shusshu* derive, in other words, from Nao's particular vision of reality rather than from traditional folk religious belief. As forms of symbolic action grounded in Nao's world view, the *shusshu* thus served to demonstrate and clarify the principal tenets of her teachings in experiential (and so concrete and visible) terms more easily understood by her followers. For example, Nao believed that Ushitora-no-Konjin, prior to revealing himself through her *kamigakari*, had remained "hidden" from the world for thousands of years, "protecting his children from behind the scenes." Because the world had now degenerated to the point where "unseen protection was no longer useful," he had decided to re-enter the world through Nao in order to carry out his plan of world reconstruction and salvation. It is in this sense that Nao saw her own mission as one of "putting Ushitora-no-Konjin back into the world" to make people aware of his true character and intentions and to convert them to faith in his saving power. In the summer of 1900, Nao identified Ushitora-no-Konjin's former dwelling place, the place where he had remained hidden for so long, as the island of Meshima.[25] By associating the *kami* with a specific place, she made the otherwise vague notion that Ushitora-no-Konjin had "come from the northeast direction" more concrete. As one might expect, Meshima is located to the northeast of Ayabe. Nao's pilgrimage to Meshima and her establishment there of a shrine to Ushitora-no-Konjin thus represented the symbolic or ritual enactment of her mission: by identifying Meshima as a sacred place and going there to "open" the island, she put Ushitora-no-Konjin back into the world and situated him more firmly in the experience and consciousness of her followers.

After the completion of the Meshima *shusshu*, Nao wrote in her *Ofudesaki* that "Meshima is a place uninhabited by human beings where the real *kami* has lived since ancient times. The opening of Meshima and Oshima has been accomplished with his help, for it concerns the reconstruction of this world" (*Keireki no shinyu*, part II, p. 5). In conducting the *shusshu*, therefore, Nao believed that she and her followers were taking necessary steps toward the achievement of the reconstruction of the world. In this respect, the explicit purpose of the *shusshu* was to assist Ushitora-no-Konjin in his efforts to destroy the present evil world and establish a new divine kingdom in its place. As the ritual means for realizing this goal, the *shusshu* were not just pilgrimages to sacred places or opportunities to engage in *shugyō*. They were also, and perhaps more importantly, sacred missions intended to insure and even hasten the reconstruction of the world. Although the *shusshu* differ in their particular activities and immediate objectives, all are informed by and contribute to this ultimate goal. Consequently, these pilgrimages had soteriological significance at the cosmic as well as personal level: as *shugyō*, the *shusshu* guaranteed the salvation of the individual participant, but as sacred missions

---

[25] Nao identified Oshima as the entrance to the dragon palace of Ryūgū-no-Otohime, a deity who was exiled to the bottom of the sea near Oshima because of his excessive greed. According to Nao, however, Ryūgū had reformed and converted to faith in Ushitora-no-Konjin. Moreover, he had pledged to use his vast "treasure" to help Ushitora-no-Konjin reconstruct the world (Yasumaru, 1977:147). Ryūgū is thus symbolic of the ideal convert to Ōmoto: one who reforms his ways and devotes himself to service to Ushitora-no-Konjin. Although Oshima is thus identified as a sacred place in Nao's scheme, Meshima is believed to be even more sacred.

Meshima Island

Commemorative photograph taken after the completion of the first Meshima shusshu (July, 1900). Seated (starting from the left) are Sumi, Nao and Onisaburō.

associated with the reconstruction, they guaranteed the salvation of the world.

The *shusshu* did not only serve, however, to demonstrate and clarify Nao's world view in a more concrete, yet symbolic, form. At the same time, they served to validate the eschatological and utopian aspects of that world view by intensifying the millenarian aspirations of Nao's followers. Because her followers shared her faith in the soteriological significance and effectiveness of the *shusshu*, participation in these missions (or even just the knowledge that they had been successfully completed by Nao) engendered a powerful sense of urgency and impending crisis (everyone must prepare for the imminent destruction of the world) and inspired absolute confidence in Nao's prediction that this crisis would be followed by a new and better life for the faithful. As specific action aimed at the transformation of this world into an ideal one, the *shusshu* thus gave Nao's millennial vision a greater immediacy and reality: the new social order she and her followers desired was no longer an uncertain and remote possibility, but a new sacred community that, through their own efforts as well as those of Ushitora-no-Konjin, would soon be established.

Through the performance of the *shusshu*, Nao was able to reassert her authority over her followers and channel their moods, beliefs, and behavior in directions which conformed to her teachings. They obeyed her every proscription, wearing only traditional Japanese cotton clothing and straw sandals because she forbade Western style clothing. At her insistence, they also stopped using tobacco and matches, ate no meat, and neither combed nor cut their hair (Yasumaru, 1977:205). Moreover, they took Nao's metaphorical descriptions of the present world literally, carrying lanterns at noon because she said the world was "dark" and walking on their hands through the streets because she said the world was "upside-down" (Yasumaru, 1977:184). It is not just a coincidence, then, that the *shusshu* were conducted and became a primary focus of belief and action during that period in Ōmoto's history when it developed into a radical millenarian cult. Indeed, the *shusshu* were largely responsible for this millennial frenzy in that they both inspired and reinforced it.

The following incident, which occurred in 1902, illustrates the religious zeal of Nao's followers and reveals her success in wresting control of the group from Onisaburō. When Nao's granddaughter, Naohi, was born, Nao refused to have her vaccinated. Nao believed that vaccinations were polluted: not only did the serum come from cows, but it had been developed in a foreign country. The Deguchis were accordingly fined for breaking the law. This enraged Nao and her followers, who demonstrated in front of city hall and police headquarters, demanding that the laws be revised and insisting that the people listen to the laws of Ushitora-no-Konjin. The local officials threatened to dispatch soldiers if they did not pay the fine, but Nao's followers just replied, "Who will be stronger -- man or *kami*?" When no one came to collect the fine, the group attributed their victory to the power of Ushitora-no-Konjin. They later discovered, however, that Onisaburō had secretly paid the fine to avoid any further confrontations with the authorities. The group angrily denounced his lack of faith (Yasumaru, 1977:185).

Although Onisaburō remained with the group and was a primary participant in the *shusshu*, he strongly opposed the anti-modern and eschatological aspects of Nao's doctrine. He viewed Nao's condemnation of all things modern or western in origin as absurd superstitions and ultimately detrimental to Japanese progress. He believed that the adoption of foreign ideas and practices was in fact necessary to the development and future prosperity of the Japanese nation. Whereas Nao insisted that modern civilization and industrialization were contrary to the will of the gods, Onisaburō argued that they conformed exactly to the divine way of "creation and growth" (*seisei ka-iku*). In this respect, his thought followed that of the Kokugaku scholars with whom he had studied. Furthermore, the well educated Onisaburō did not agree with Nao that the use of *kanji* (Chinese ideographs) was "injurious to the nation" (Nao wrote her *Ofudesaki* almost entirely in *kana*, or Japanese phonetic symbols) or that "schools were necessarily evil" (Yasumaru, 1977:186-187).

What Onisaburō found most disturbing about Nao's teachings, however, was her belief that the complete destruction of the world would precede the establishment of a divine realm on earth. After 1900, Nao's *Ofudesaki* became increasingly eschatological in content and tone as she described in detail the catastrophes which would befall the world if people did not reform. Nao predicted that there would be a great war and devastating earthquakes. For three days the sun would not shine and it would rain fire. Even Tokyo would be attacked, leaving nothing but a field of pampas grass.[26] Those who did not appeal to *kami* would be thrown into deep ravines as an example to others. These catastrophic events would reduce the population of the world by two-thirds. Finally, the world would become a muddy ocean, for, from the nothingness of a muddy ocean, *kami*

---

[26] These prophecies, like other aspects of Nao's *Ofudesaki*, have been subjected to reinterpretation. Ōmoto followers today credit Nao with having predicted the nuclear devastation of Hiroshima and Nagasaki in 1945.

had first created the world and now he would do it again (quoted in Yasumaru, 1977:184, 187-188, 213-214).

Despite Onisaburō's criticism that such threatening language only served to deceive the people, Nao's followers took her predictions literally and were convinced that the end of the world was near. As described above, participation in the *shusshu* both stimulated and reinforced this simultaneous sense of impending doom and imminent salvation. This sense, in turn, lent a greater immediacy and urgency to Nao's constant insistence that her followers obey the will of *kami* and reform and work quickly to persuade others to do the same. Thus, under Nao's dominant influence, the group developed into a fanatic millenarian cult whose members believed that Ushitora-no-Konjin would soon destroy the present evil world and establish a new divine realm in its place (Yasumaru, 1977:188).

This phase of millennial frenzy reached its peak during the Russo-Japanese War. After Japan declared war on Russia in February, 1904, Nao predicted that the Japanese would suffer a crushing defeat at the hands of the Russians and that this defeat would mark the beginning of the end of the world. As the war proceeded, even though a series of successful land battles made a Japanese victory almost certain, the belief that the reconstruction of the world would soon be realized further intensified among Nao and her followers. In response to these rising expectations, on May 14, 1905, Nao initiated the final *shusshu*. With her son, Denkichi, and another male follower, she again travelled to Meshima where she stayed for twelve days, worshipping Ushitora-no-Konjin at the shrine and praying for the reconstruction. It was a difficult vigil, for the island lacked both fresh water and vegetation and she and her two companions had no shelter from the wind and rain. But Nao's efforts and prayers proved futile. On May 27, 1905, the day after she returned to Ayabe, the Japanese fleet intercepted and destroyed the Russian Baltic fleet in the Straits of Tsushima. Contrary to Nao's predictions, the Japanese had won the war and the result was not devastation, but increased national pride and prosperity.

Nao's prophecies concerning the end of the world had failed before, but this time, her disillusioned followers refused to accept her explanation that Ushitora-no-Konjin had compassionately decided at the last minute to give people more time to reform before carrying out the reconstruction of the world in order to avoid too drastic a reduction in the population (Yasumaru, 1977:214). Angered by this betrayal of their millennial hopes, the group broke up, leaving only Nao, Onisaburō, Sumi, Nao's younger sister, and Onisaburō's mother (Yasumaru, 1977:226). Thus, in May, 1905, the most radical millenarian period in Ōmoto's history came to an abrupt and dramatic close. Having lost her credibility, Nao was never again able to assert her own authority over the group and Onisaburō took control of doctrinal and organizational matters. This shift in leadership was formalized in 1910 when Onisaburō officially succeeded to the headship of the Deguchi household.

In 1906, Onisaburō went to Kyoto where he enrolled as a student at the Institute for the Study of the Japanese Classics (Kōten Kōkyūkō-sho). Two years later, after being ordained as a Shinto priest and serving for several months at a shrine in Kyoto, he returned to Ayabe and established a new religious organization under the auspices of Taiseikyō, one of the thirteen Shinto sects officially recognized by the Meiji government.[27] This new group, called the Dainihon Shusai-kai, stressed the importance of reverence for the Emperor and explicitly supported the nationalistic doctrines of State Shinto. Its annual calendar of events focused on festivals associated with the imperial cult and Japanese nationalism. Onisaburō's well organized proselytizing efforts were very successful: he was able to acquire the financial backing of several influential people and by 1912 had increased his following in the Ayabe area to almost one thousand members (Yasumaru, 1977:226-228).

In spite of Ōmoto's rapid development during the Taishō period, Nao sank into a deep depression in the last years of her life. Under Onisaburō's leadership, the group had taken a course far different from the one she had envisioned. Nao and her *Ofudesaki*, once the central focus of the group's belief and practice, were now eclipsed by Onisaburō and his nationalistic Shinto doctrines, spiritualistic practices, and theories of modern civilization. Although Nao continued to threaten a catastrophic end to the world if people did not act in accordance with her teachings, she was no longer taken seriously. In 1918, at the age of 81, agonized by her belief that she had failed to fulfill her mission to reconstruct the world and angry that she had not yet been compensated for her matchless suffering, Nao died (Yasumaru, 1977:215).

---

[27] Taiseikyō was founded by a former samurai, Hirayama Seisai (1815-1890). Its doctrines were based on Confucian ethical teachings and traditional Shinto beliefs and practices. Its adherents engaged in purification ceremonies, horoscopy, divination, and rites of meditation. The group was involved in the traditional Japanese arts and explicitly supported advancements in science and business, interests which Onisaburō shared.

Deguchi Nao

III
A New Vision of Reality: Structure and Content

> If anything is heightened in the ecstatic interlude, it is the cognitive faculties of the mystic: he knows something that others do not know and that he did not know before... he has, for the first time, seen things as they really are (Greeley, 1974:4).

This is precisely what Nao discovered in her experience of *kamigakari* and recorded in the *Ofudesaki*: a radically new knowledge of the way things really are, have been and will be. She wrote that there are those who think "all is right with the world," but they are simply "deaf and blind" to the truth. They do not see that the present world is "thoroughly under the sway of evil spirits" (5/5/1898; Hino, 1974:21) and has become a "dark and devilish place" in which human beings are no more than "monsters and fierce beasts -- the stronger preying upon the weaker" (1/1892; Hino, 1974:1).[28] Society has been turned "upside-down" -- that which is evil now appears good and that which is wrong is regarded as right. Those spirits and people who "have hitherto held the reins of government, knowing nothing, have ruined and devastated the world..." (7/12/1893; Hino, 1974:6). Now the world is so "defiled and disgraced by evil" that "it cannot go one inch further" (1904; Deguchi, 1977:71). It is on the verge of "collapsing into a muddy tract of desolation and mankind is on the brink of total extinction" (4/1898; Hino, 1974:35).

---

[28] In this chapter, references to quotes from Nao's *Ofudesaki* will include the date (according to the lunar calendar) she recorded it, and the author, publication date and page number of the book where it is cited.

But Nao's teachings include a message of hope as well as despair, for Ushitora-no-Konjin, the creator and protector of the world, manifested himself through Deguchi Nao to save it from total destruction. He will reconstruct "this chaotic world into a crystal-clear one, separating good from evil and judging right from wrong" (1899; Miyata, 1975:237). He will establish a divine kingdom on earth in which all people will be equal and live in "peace and harmony forever." This promise of salvation is not, however, an unconditional one. Only those who have absolute faith in Ushitora-no-Konjin and reform themselves in accordance with his teachings will be saved. The *Ofudesaki* thus repeatedly warns its readers of the horrible disasters that will befall them if they do not repent, correct their evil ways and purify their spirits.

This, in brief outline, is the central message of Nao's teachings -- the new vision of reality she discovered in an altered state of consciousness. It is an inherently religious view of the world, for it attributes meaning to human experience with reference to an ultimate conception of sacred order and divine authority. At the same time, however, it had important political implications, for, as we have seen, Nao explicitly rejected the ideology of the Meiji State and projected a vision of a new social order in conflict with the government's central aims. Furthermore, in voicing her own dissatisfaction and utopian aspirations, Nao spoke for a class of people severely dislocated by socioeconomic changes in late nineteenth century Japan -- for those excluded, in other words, from Meiji "progress."

So far, in an effort to establish both the personal and larger sociocultural contexts of Nao's world view, I have discussed her teachings in a necessarily piecemeal fashion. In this chapter, however, I shall consider her world view and the religious action she prescribed as a structurally integrated whole. Of course, such a totalizing and synchronic mode of analysis presents a systematic objectification of Nao's teachings of which she herself was not conscious. As she struggled over a period of many years to elaborate on her initial revelations and communicate her new vision of reality to others, Nao gradually incorporated various symbols, ideas and modes of action into her teachings. She thus formulated and articulated her world view in practice rather than through the systematic construction of general theories. Yet, in spite of this slow process of appropriation and synthesis, her teachings manifest a striking coherency. This is because her thinking was structured in terms of two fundamental paradigms. One is associated with Shinto notions of purity and pollution and the other with Buddhist millenarian beliefs which include eschatological and utopian elements. Each of these paradigms provided Nao with a conceptual framework and a language to articulate, organize and evaluate her own experience and the world around her. Although both paradigms are derived from Japanese folk religion, they are significantly transformed within the context of Nao's thought.

Before we can proceed, however, with this analysis of Nao's world view and the paradigms which informed its construction, it is necessary to discuss briefly the texts from which it is drawn. The major source of our knowledge of Nao's teachings is her collected writings, the *Ofudesaki*. Unfortunately, the manner in which this text was written and later transcribed, preserved, and suppressed poses serious problems of interpretation. The original version of the *Ofudesaki* is virtually illegible. Nao recorded each entry in a trance-like state, writing energetically and with great speed. Her writing implements were of the crudest sort because her followers could barely afford the paper, brushes, and ink that she used in such large quantities. Except for the occasional phonetic use of numbers (for example, "Deguchi" is sometimes written with the Chinese character for "nine"), she wrote entirely in *hiragana* (phonetic syllables) and rarely punctuated her sentences. Even Nao's closest followers had great difficulty deciphering her writings. At her insistence, however, and with the help of her detailed explanations, a few were able to copy her writings into a more legible form. Although parts of Nao's original version have survived, most of the existing manuscript of the *Ofudesaki* (or what remains of it -- a large part was lost or confiscated by the police over the years) was copied in this way (Yasumaru, 1977:104). In conducting the research for this paper, I did not have access to these manuscripts, but relied instead on several different published editions of Nao's writings. In what follows, I will briefly discuss these editions and their value as sources for our understanding of Nao's thought.[29]

---

[29] In 1982, San'ichi Shobō published the first volume of *Ōmoto shiryō shūsei*, a three volume collection of excerpts from the writings of Nao and Onisaburō. Edited by Ikeda Akira, it is the first such collection to be published by an outside press (previous editions of the founders' writings have all been published by Ōmotokyō). The first 832 pages of the *Ōmoto shiryō shūsei* are devoted to excerpts from Nao's *Ofudesaki*. These excerpts are arranged chronologically by entry date, that is, in the order Nao recorded them in her *Ofudesaki*. Unfortunately, I did not discover the existence of this collection until the summer of 1983, by which time I had already completed the research for (and much of the writing of) the thesis on which this book is based. Fortunately, the excerpts are taken from the same previously published editions of the *Ofudesaki* I used. Because I have included the date of entry when quoting from Nao's writings, readers interested in the original Japanese can consult the *Ōmoto shiryō shūsei* if they do not have access to these earlier editions.

Excerpts from Nao's *Ofudesaki* were first published in 1917, the year before her death. Selected and transcribed by Onisaburō, these excerpts appeared in the group's monthly magazine, *Shinreikai*, from February of that year until March, 1920. Passages from the *Ofudesaki* were also included in the first four issues published in 1921. In 1919, a small collection of Nao's writings selected from back issues of *Shinreikai* was published separately under the title *Ōmoto shinyu ten no maki*. The following year, Onisaburō published another collection of excerpts from the *Ofudesaki*. These, too, had already appeared in issues of *Shinreikai*. Called the *Ōmoto shinyu hi no maki*, this volume contained several passages which explicitly condemned the government and the Emperor. As a result, it was officially banned soon after its publication. The government suppression of Ōmotokyō in 1922 has been attributed in part to the publication of this book as it created, for the first time in the history of the group, a broad public awareness of Nao's harsh social criticism and radical religious teachings (Yasumaru, 1977:107). In 1977, the Education Department of Ōmotokyō published in a single volume all the excerpts from the *Ofudesaki* which had appeared in *Shinreikai*. This book, called the *Hyō no shinyu*, is particularly useful because the original printing plates were used in its production.

Although the Taishō editions of Nao's *Ofudesaki* are considered to be very close to the original, there are still some significant differences which must be taken into account when using them as a source for understanding Nao's thought. In this context, it should be recalled that the *Ofudesaki* is essentially an orally transmitted text: directly inspired by Nao's experience of *kamigakari*, it retains the quality and form of spoken rather than written discourse. This is most evident in the grammatical errors, redundancies, and inexplicable leaps from one subject to another which mark the text as well as in the use of peculiar pronunciations and colloquial expressions characteristic of the Tamba dialect Nao spoke. As Yasumaru (1977:105) has described it, the *Ofudesaki* "represents the expression, without embellishment or ordering, of thoughts which gushed out naturally as the words of *kami*." This does not mean, however, that the *Ofudesaki* lacks an explicit and well structured world view. To the contrary, as I indicated above, Nao's thought is internally consistent and coherent in spite of the spontaneous and rather chaotic form of its presentation.

According to Ōmoto tradition, Onisaburō was the only person who could actually read and fully understand Nao's writings. However, in preparing her *Ofudesaki* for publication, he had to break her prose into grammatical sentences and logical paragraphs and transcribe the *hiragana* (phonetic symbols) into Chinese characters (*kanji*) in order to make the text comprehensible to the average reader. Although the resulting changes in the original text usually function to clarify what Nao intended to say, there are passages where Onisaburō clearly changed the original meaning of the text. As I indicated earlier, Onisaburō was a highly educated man whose interests and opinions often diverged radically from Nao's. According to Yasumaru, Onisaburō added his own concerns and knowledge to Nao's in rewriting her *Ofudesaki*. His influence is most apparent in those sections of the Taishō editions which are too theologically sophisticated to have been written by Nao (Yasumaru, 1977:85). Furthermore, in interpreting these editions of Nao's writings, one must avoid attributing too much importance to particular *kanji*, for the Chinese characters Onisaburō chose to replace Nao's *hiragana* often add new or unintended meanings and allusions to the words Nao used.

The issue of Onisaburō's influence becomes even more problematic when one considers the most easily available edition of the *Ofudesaki*, the *Ōmoto shinyu*. This five volume collection of Nao's writings is one of Ōmotokyō's two canonical texts (the other is Onisaburō's *Reikai monogatari*). Ōmoto adherents today believe that it contains the true words of *kami* (expressed through Nao), whereas Nao's other writings represent her own words or those of other (lesser) gods and spirits. The *Ōmoto shinyu* was first compiled after World War II by Onisaburō and (following his death in 1948) by two of his closest disciples. It consists of selections from the *Ofudesaki* which had already been published, primarily in the Taishō editions discussed above. Ōmotokyō published the present edition in 1968. Although the *Ōmoto shinyu* is easier to read than any of the earlier editions of Nao's writings, it should not be used as the sole source for the interpretation and analysis of Nao's thought. This is because Onisaburō systematically excluded from this edition any passages which were explicitly critical of the Japanese government or Emperor. He had good reasons for doing so. In 1935, Ōmotokyō had again been subjected to severe government suppression. The group's headquarters in Ayabe and Kameoka were destroyed and Onisaburō, along with several of his closest followers, was arrested. Convicted of lèse majesté and violation of the Peace Maintenance Law, he was sentenced to life imprisonment. He was released, however, in 1942, and in 1945 the charges against him were formally dropped. Even so, in reestablishing Ōmotokyō after the war, Onisaburō believed it was still necessary to adopt a more politically cautious stance toward the government. This included the elimination of those passages from published editions of Nao's writings which had formerly incurred the wrath of the government authorities.

Although the *Ōmoto shinyu* provides little insight into the sociopolitical dimensions of Nao's world view, it remains a useful source for understanding the eschatological and utopian aspects of her teachings as well as her use of Shinto notions of purity and pollution. In the analysis of Nao's new vision of reality which follows, I quote extensively from Hino Iwao's translation of excerpts from the *Ōmoto shinyu*. Apart from its sometimes flowery language and failure to really capture the more strident tone of the original *Ofudesaki*, this translation is an accurate one. I also cite passages from the *Ofudesaki* (which I translated myself) quoted in studies of Ōmotokyō by Yasumaru Yoshio, Miyata Noboru, and Kozawa Hiroshi. These scholars have, for the most part, relied on the Taishō editions of Nao's writings.

One other collection of excerpts from the *Ofudesaki* which I have found especially useful is the *Keireki no shinyu*. It was compiled between 1961 and 1963 by Deguchi Uchimarō, one of Onisaburō's foremost disciples and the husband of his daughter (and Nao's granddaughter), Naohi. At that time, Ōmotokyō headquarters was conducting research on the group's history with the assistance of several Japanese scholars of popular religion. The result of their collaboration was the publication, in 1964, of the two volume *Ōmoto nanajūnen-shi (The Seventy-year History of Ōmoto)*. Intended as an aid to the researchers, the *Keireki no shinyu* was Uchimarō's contribution to this project. As the title suggests (*keireki* means "personal history"), it is primarily a collection of Nao's reflections on her own life. It also includes, however, passages which refer to Nao's personal and doctrinal conflicts with Onisaburō and her views of the Russo-Japanese War. In addition, one long section is devoted to Nao's interpretations of the *shusshu*, the pilgrimages she and her followers conducted between 1900 and 1905. Uchimarō selected these passages from unpublished manuscripts as well as published editions of Nao's writings.

It is only through the composite reading and careful interpretation of the above editions of Nao's *Ofudesaki* that an accurate account of her world view is possible. In the analysis which follows of Nao's new vision of reality, I shall first place her radical millenarianism in a larger theoretical and historical context before proceeding to a discussion of the content and paradigmatic structure of her thought and the forms of religious action she created.

Millenarianism

Throughout this book, I have described Nao's world view and the cult she founded as essentially millenarian. In this respect, my position is the same as that of two scholars of Japanese popular religion, Miyata Noboru and Yasumaru Yoshio. According to Miyata (1975:234), millenarian beliefs hold a "pivotal position" in Nao's teachings. Yasumaru agrees with this assessment, but claims further that Ōmotokyō represents the most complete development of millenarian thought in Japanese history (1977:10). How is the term "millenarian" being used here and what is the particular form that such beliefs and practices have taken in Japan?

The term "millenarian" originally referred to a particular variant of Christian eschatology. In most anthropological and historical scholarship of the last three decades, however, it has come to have a more general meaning. Norman Cohn, for example, in his comprehensive history of European millenarian movements, argues that it has become "a convenient label for a particular type of salvationism" (1974:15). He goes on to define millenarian movements or sects as those which picture salvation as

a) collective, in the sense that it is to be enjoyed by the faithful as a collectivity;

b) terrestrial, in the sense that it is to be realized on this earth;

c) imminent, in the sense that it is to come both soon and suddenly;

d) total, in the sense that it is utterly to transform life on earth so that the new dispensation will be no mere improvement on the present, but perfection itself; and

e) miraculous, in the sense that it is to be accomplished by, or with the help of, supernatural agencies (Cohn, 1974:15).

Although this definition does provide an accurate description of how millenarian movements in general (and Nao's cult in particular) view salvation, it fails to account for other important dimensions of such movements. As many scholars of the subject agree, millenarian movements or sects are fundamentally protests against oppression (in its ideological as well as economic and political forms) and attempts to construct a new kind of community in which no such oppression will exist. They accordingly arise among people who perceive themselves as subject to an unjust and impersonal authority; as objects or pawns in someone else's game (Douglas, 1970:175-184). Participants in millenarian movements also share an awareness of being disenfranchised; that is, separated from the mainstream of power and its associated activities (Burridge, 1969:105). This accounts for what Peter Worsley has called "the anti-authoritarian attitude" of millenarian movements and sects (1968:225-226). This attitude is found not only in the rejection of prevailing social, economic and political institutions (in the new society to come, there will be no human rulers or judges, no policemen, landlords or merchants), but also in the projection of a world view in direct conflict with the ideology of the ruling authorities. In other words, as E.J. Hobsbawm has argued, millenarian movements must be considered as revolutionary movements, for they represent "a profound and total rejection of the present, evil world and a passionate longing for another, better one" (1965:57). Whereas reformists accept the existing social order and seek only to improve it, revolutionaries believe it must be radically transformed and even abolished (Hobsbawm, 1965:10-11). So, too, in the millenarian world view, the existing social order is harshly criticized and ultimately emptied of all positive value. While awaiting its imminent destruction, participants instead affirm the new social order which is to replace it. Millenarian movements and sects thus function to dissociate participants from, rather than integrate them into, the existing social order.

This sociopolitical dimension is present in millenarian movements and sects even when (as is usually the case) they fail to develop an effective political organization or specific strategy for achieving a radical transformation of the social order. "The followers of millenarian movements are not makers of revolution. They expect it to make itself (by divine intervention, miracle, etc.)" (Hobsbawm 1965:58). Meanwhile, they gather together "to watch the signs of the coming doom, to listen to the prophets who predict the coming of the great day" and to undertake certain ritual measures to prepare themselves for admission to the future heaven on earth (Hobsbawm, 1965:59). The point is, however, that millenarian movements are fundamentally efforts to radically alter the oppressive socioeconomic and political circumstances in which their followers find themselves. Although the means they employ to realize this goal may not include conventional political resistance, it cannot be denied that the world views they provide are revolutionary in the ideological sense of the term. Nor does the fact that these world views are articulated in the language of apocalyptic and utopian religion mean that we must define millenarian movements and sects as primarily religious rather than sociopolitical phenomena. First of all, such an interpretation relies on a far too narrow (even naive) understanding of "religion" and "politics" per se. Secondly, those communities in which millenarian movements arise do not themselves make clear distinctions between the religious and the secular. Thus, "to argue whether such a sect is religious or social is meaningless, for it will automatically and always be both in some manner" (Hobsbawm, 1965:66).

Similarly, one should beware of reducing millenarian movements to mere emotional (and thus ineffectual) responses to poverty, social change and oppression or seeing them only as a final resort to irrational beliefs and practices in the face of utter despair. Although millenarian movements do indeed fulfill compelling emotional needs and engender powerful emotional states, they always have an important cognitive or conceptual dimension as well. According to K.O.L. Burridge, millenarian movements and sects are actually "new cultures in the making"; attempts, in other words, "to construct a new kind of society or moral community" (1968:8). Their leaders articulate shared, but latent, aspirations to break out of existing patterns of socioeconomic relations and political domination and establish a new social order founded on different principles. Perceiving that their former values, assumptions and categories can no longer meaningfully account for experience in a changing social environment, they set themselves the task of reformulating their assumptions and constructing a new system of values and categories which can explain experience and serve as an effective guide for conduct (Burridge, 1969:10). Millenarian movements and sects thus constitute an intellectually constructive and culturally innovative response to oppression and social change. Neither the leaders nor the followers of these movements are the unfortunate victims of irrational fantasies. They are, rather, individuals who, conscious of their economic, political and ideological oppression, are trying to work out in religious terms viable solutions to their problems.

This effort to construct a new system of values and categories also gives millenarian movements and sects an important moral dimension. They are concerned not only with the nature of "truth" and legitimate authority, but also with the distinction between good and evil, right and wrong. In this context, Burridge has argued that the problem of personal integrity, of what it means to be "human," is central to all millenarian movements (1969:11). As Douglas has observed, millenarian sects arise in situations where people feel excluded, disregarded and of little or no value (1970:66). "What they experience," she argues, "is a failure to recognize their claims as persons" (1970:181). The formulation of a new morality or ethical system aims, therefore, not only to create a more humane and egalitarian society, but also to resolve the strongly felt need for new sources of self-respect and new measures of social prestige. Participants in millenarian movements generally reject the accumulation of material wealth as the primary determinant of social status and instead envision a very simple society in which there will be no need for money; a social order in which moral virtue, not material wealth, is the measure of human worth. To quote Peter Worsley, "the moralities of plainness, simplicity, frugality, and asceticism" characteristic of most millenarian movements "are not just the creations of poor men making a virtue of necessity and a creed out of sour grapes. They imply the rejection of a temporal order that makes the pleasures of the flesh the goals of human striving" (1968:254).

More specifically, when millenarian movements arise in complex and rapidly modernizing societies, this desire for simplicity, frugality, and a new moral order also implies the rejection of both a developing capitalist system and increasing government intervention in people's everyday lives. In his study of revolutionary social movements in Europe (most of which manifest millenarian aspirations and symbols), E.J. Hobsbawm found that they usually occurred in situations where modern capitalism had recently "irrupted" into a peasant society (1965:67). In these communities, the people saw themselves as the objects of insidious socioeconomic forces which they could neither understand nor control (1965:3). Land reforms, including the abolition of common forest and pasture lands, increased taxes, rapid industrialization, the development of a national market, and the introduction of capitalist legal and social relationships all had "cataclysmic effects" on these societies (1965:67-68). According to Hobsbawm, the participants in the revolutionary movements he studied did not grow with or into modern society; instead, they were "broken into it." Their problem was "how to adapt themselves to its life and struggles" (1965:3). Millenarian movements thus constitute one mode of response to oppressive and rapid socioeconomic change: participants not only reject the capitalist system imposed on them from the outside, but also construct a vision of a new social order which embodies their own concerns and aspirations.

It is in reference to this particular understanding of millenarianism, one derived from the work of Hobsbawm, Worsley, Burridge, Douglas, and Cohn, that I have identified Nao's world view and the cult she established as fundamentally millenarian in content and structure, theory and practice. In this respect, Nao's cult as it developed between 1892 and 1905 represents the only case of a full-blown millenarian movement in Japanese history. Although millenarian notions are present in the Japanese Buddhist canonical tradition, in various folk religious beliefs and practices and in many nineteenth century peasant uprisings, these constitute only partial appropriations of millenarian symbols. The distinction I am making here is between those social phenomena which contain millenarian elements and those which are, in accordance with the above definition, millenarian movements or sects. It is useful, in analyzing this distinction, to consider millenarianism as a conceptual paradigm which embodies specific assumptions and can serve to structure and evaluate reality in a particular way. In essence, it provides a simple system of classification which is grounded in the fundamental duality between good and evil. This duality is the source of the basic opposition between the negatively valued present and the positively valued future -- between this world and the new one to come -- characteristic of all millenarian thought. The paradigm further focuses attention on the horizontality rather than verticality of human relationships. Only relationships between human beings and the gods are conceived in hierarchical terms. This gives rise to an emphasis on the equality of human beings and the concomitant rejection of a hierarchically organized social order. It is for this reason that millenarian movements often call for a "leveling" of society. Finally, the paradigm involves a notion of sacred authority and divine righteousness which transcends existing authority structures and can thus pass judgement on them. As a particular conceptual mode for making sense of experience, therefore, the millenarian paradigm not only channels utopian aspirations, but also allows for harsh criticism of the status quo. In this latter respect, it easily serves as a source of divine legitimation for revolutionary creeds and actions. It can be used, moreover, to explain suffering and account for natural calamities (usually read as signs of the imminent end of the world). When I speak, then, of the millenarian paradigm, I am using the term "paradigm" in J.G.A. Pocock's sense of a "reference point within the structure of consciousness stable and durable enough to be used at more than one moment and so by more than one actor in more than one way" (1973:280).

The millenarian paradigm dominated Nao's thinking about the world: it constituted the fundamental conceptual framework within which she structured her vision of reality, articulated her aspirations, and resolved her concerns. One can identify other social and religious movements in Japanese history which contain millenarian elements, but in these movements the paradigm plays an auxiliary rather than central role. In other words, the symbols and language of the millenarian paradigm are employed to reinforce or expand on ideas generated within a different conceptual framework. This means that the logical implications of the paradigm are never fully explored or addressed as they are in a radical millenarian cult like Nao's. Consequently, these kinds of movements generally lack one or more of the moral, cognitive, and sociopolitical dimensions I described above as characteristic of millenarian movements and sects. The following brief survey of various manifestations of millenarian symbols and aspirations in Japan will help to clarify my use of the "millenarian paradigm." At the same time, it will show how Nao's teachings and cult both draw on and go beyond the tradition of millennial thought and action in Japan.

Buddhism, like Christianity, has a doctrine of a future messiah. This is the Bodhisattva Maitreya (Miroku, in Japanese) who, at the end of the Latter Days of the Dharma (*Mappō*) will descend from his present abode in the Tsuita Heaven[30] and re-establish the Buddhist Law on earth. Based on this scriptural tradition, devotion to Maitreya evolved in two different directions, one embodying millennial aspirations and the other not. In the latter case, devotees focused their energies on acquiring sufficient merit to be reborn in Maitreya's Tsuita Heaven, much as Pure Land followers hoped for rebirth in Amida's heavenly paradise. In the former case, however, devotees stressed Maitreya's role as the future Buddha or savior who was to descend from the Tsuita Heaven to establish his paradise on earth. Although the coming of Maitreya was usually consigned to the distant future, at certain points in Japanese history his arrival was believed to be imminent.

The cult of Maitreya was brought to Japan in the early sixth century, but received little attention until the Heian Period (794-1133) when it became popular among the aristocracy. The story of Kūkai, founder of Shingon Buddhism, shows how both forms of the Maitreya cult could find expression in Japan. Before he died in 835, Kūkai proclaimed that he would surely be reborn in the Tsuita Heaven from where, fifty-six million years hence, he would descend with Maitreya to this world. After his death, "his fervent disciples spread the idea that Kūkai had not really died, but instead was interred upon the mountain top in a state of deep meditation (*nyūjō*)" awaiting the advent of Maitreya (Miyata, 1983:7). Although examples such as this of belief in Maitreya's coming as well as many artistic representations of the Bodhisattva can be found in medieval Japan, it was not until the Tokugawa period that millennial beliefs and practices associated with the Maitreya cult became a common feature of Japanese folk

---

[30] According to Buddhist cosmology, the Tsuita Heaven is the fourth of the six heavens in the *Kamadhatu* or "world of desire." With the rise of the Mahayana tradition, belief in a number of "pure lands" (or Buddha fields) developed. Each field or "heaven" was associated with a different Bodhisattva. See Sponberg and Hardacre, *Maitreya, the Future Buddha* (1988), for a comprehensive, cross-cultural analysis of Maitreya/Miroku beliefs and practices.

religion. This popularization of belief in "Miroku" and his paradise was accomplished primarily by ascetic priests (*yamabushi*) who organized cults centered on the worship of sacred mountains. The direct association made during the Heian Period between the idea of *Mappō* and belief in Miroku's advent also continued in the Tokugawa period. Talk of the advent of Miroku usually increased in years of grave famines or epidemics because it was believed that such difficult times were a sign that the *Miroku-no-yo* (the world of Miroku) was about to begin.

For example, in the villages along the eastern coast of Japan, from Ibaragi to Shizuoka Prefecture, songs were sung on certain occasions which predicted the coming of Miroku's ship. The ship would be laden with rice and its arrival would usher in an era of bountiful harvests. Special dances (*Miroku odori*) were performed in conjunction with these songs. These beliefs and practices were strongest in the area around the Kashima shrine. An oracle given annually by the priestess of this shrine was believed to invoke the *Miroku-no-yo*, a world of extraordinary fertility and abundance. Within the ritual complex, the songs heralded the coming of Miroku and the agrarian utopia he would establish. The dances served to purify the world and to ward off evils such as famines and epidemics. Japanese folklorists have determined that these beliefs and practices, which may still be found today, probably first appeared sometime in the eighteenth century (Miyata, 1983:10-12).

Whereas the Kashima cult to Miroku located his residence somewhere across the sea, in other parts of Japan he was believed to reside at the tops of sacred mountains. In a practice that echoes the legend of Kūkai's interment on Mt. Koya, some priests associated with eighteenth and nineteenth century mountain cults chose to achieve self-mummification through slow fasting. They hoped to use the sacred power they would accumulate through such severe austerities to benefit others. It was believed, moreover, that they did not actually die, but entered a state of suspended animation (*nyūjō*) to await the coming of Miroku (Blacker, 1976:89).

The best known example of self-mummification is that of the sixth leader of Fuji-kō, Itō Ihei. Fuji-kō was a devotional association of laymen and women centered on the worship of Mt. Fuji. The faithful were expected to make pilgrimages to the mountain as often as possible and practice various religious austerities (either of a magical or meditative character) at its peak. Fuji-kō was established in the early eighteenth century, but grew most rapidly after Itō Ihei prophesied the advent of Miroku in 1773. When he first joined Fuji-kō, Itō was a wealthy merchant who managed an oil business in Edo. After learning the teachings of Fuji-kō and climbing the mountain many times, however, he decided to abandon his wealth and devote himself to ascetic practices on Mt. Fuji. At this point in his career, he changed his name to Miroku. In 1773, "he received an oracle from the deity of Mt. Fuji, Sengen Bosatsu, and, entering a deep meditative trance on the top of Mt. Fuji, proclaimed the advent of the *Miroku-no-yo*" (Miyata, 1983:20). There, sitting in a cave, he drank only water until he died. Itō was believed by his followers to be the messiah, the savior and the incarnation of Miroku himself. As the news of his self-mummification and prophecy spread, membership in Fuji-kō increased rapidly. By the turn of the century, there were 808 branches in Edo and the group had begun to recruit in the rural areas outside the city (Miyata, 1983:20).

Although Japanese folklorists and historians of religion have found millenarian beliefs and practices throughout Japanese history, they all agree that such occurrences were most pervasive in the nineteenth century. During this period of rapid socioeconomic change and political upheaval, the utopian aspirations of the people were expressed in a number of religious movements and movements of social protest which employed millenarian symbols. These aspirations were articulated, however, not only in terms of the imminent advent of Miroku, but also through the popular notion of *yonaoshi*, or "world renewal." As a call for a radical transformation in the social order, this slogan includes the idea of rectifying social and moral abuses and setting the world to rights again. In many cases, Miroku beliefs and *yonaoshi* slogans were used together and thus reinforced one another: references to Miroku gave divine sanction to social protest and the notion of *yonaoshi* helped to ground otherwise abstract utopian visions in a specific social reality.

In 1837, Ōshio Heihachirō led a rebellion in Osaka, claiming that he would "save the people from the hell of the past and establish paradise before their very eyes." Although he was captured and executed by the government authorities, many people believed that he had not died, but would eventually return to fulfill his promise. He became something of a cult figure and offerings were made to him at shrines throughout Japan. The millenarian aspirations Ōshio voiced and inspired are admittedly vague, but this incident was easily absorbed into a popular consciousness which was increasingly critical of the status quo and emphatically proclaimed the hope for a new and better world.

Following the Edo earthquake of 1855, *namazu-e* (woodblock prints of catfish with brief inscriptions) were widely distributed in the city.

At that time, Japanese folk belief held that earthquakes were caused by the angry thrashing about of monster-size *namazu* who lived beneath the islands of Japan. According to Ouwehand (1964:30), the prints were produced for the itinerant workers, small tradesmen and recent migrants from the countryside who composed the lower classes of Edo society. He convincingly interprets the prints as an expression of how people accounted for this devastating event. Many of the prints suggest that the earthquake was seen as righteous compensation for social and economic abuses (1964:241). For example, some prints picture the *namazu* forcing the rich to vomit up their money. The money then falls like rain into the open hands of the poor people below. But Ouwehand also found prints in which references are made to the imminent advent of the *Miroku-no-yo* and the desire for world renewal or *yonaoshi*. It seems that the *namazu* was regarded as a "helping god" who would come bearing treasures and change the world into a better, more equal and just one (Ouwehand, 1964:31). Ouwehand concludes that the earthquake was widely perceived as a turning point, the beginning of a new era in which the poor would be allowed to share in the good things which up to then had been unfairly monopolized by a small social elite (1964:237). The *namazu* prints thus show how millenarian ideas could be appropriated to account for cataclysmic events by assigning them a positive meaning. This particular explanation of the earthquake enabled the Edo poor to vent their dissatisfaction with the present social order and voice their aspirations for something better.

In addition to the *namazu-e*, the 1850s and 1860s witnessed several other popular religious movements which expressed millennial yearnings. These included mass pilgrimages to temples and shrines (*okage mairi*) and mass outbursts of frenzied dancing and singing (*eejanaika*). In 1867, reports that talismans believed to be omens of divine favor were raining down over Kyoto, Osaka, and Edo triggered a number of the latter events. Poor peasants and townspeople wandered through the countryside in large groups, begging for alms and engaging in wild and licentious behavior. Convinced that a new world was about to be established on earth, the participants proclaimed the advent of Miroku and rejoiced in their good fortune.

Millenarian aspirations and symbols can also be found in the new religions which were established in the nineteenth century. Unlike the spontaneous and short-lived *okage mairi* and *eejanaika*, these religious organizations developed permanent institutional structures and specific doctrines and rituals. Tenrikyō, one of the first of these, was founded by Nakayama Miki in 1863. Through an experience of *kamigakari*, Miki prophesied that "a heavenly dew" would fall from the sky and inaugurate a "new divine era of perfect bliss" -- the present age of misery and strife would end and the world would be born anew. Miki envisioned this new world as one in which everyone would be equal and live healthy, prosperous lives. Like Miki, the founders of the other new religions appropriated millenarian symbols and ideas to express their utopian aspirations and dissatisfaction with the present social order. However, because the millenarian paradigm played an auxiliary rather than dominant role in their thinking about the world, none of these new religions developed into a radical millenarian cult as did Nao's.

All the nineteenth century movements I have discussed up to now appropriated millenarian symbols and slogans to express their demands for social reform and emancipation from economic oppression. These demands, however, never went beyond the level of vaguely articulated aspirations for a more happy and prosperous life. Although this fact in no way detracts from their importance as movements of popular resistance, it does sharply differentiate them from the peasant uprisings (*ikki*) of the same period. The *ikki* rebels formally articulated their demands in petitions addressed to local officials. In stating their opposition to such things as increased taxes and rates of interest, universal conscription and the abuse of authority by local government officials, they made their objectives quite clear. Not content with merely voicing vague aspirations for a better society, the rebels made direct appeals for specific policy reforms and institutional changes. At the same time, however, they too appropriated millenarian symbols and slogans. In the Chichibu rebellion of 1884, for example, the rebels claimed to be agents of Miroku working to bring about the renewal of the world: the term "*yonaoshi*" was even emblazoned on their banners. According to Irwin Scheiner, the leaders of this rebellion saw it as their sacred mission to change the world and make all people equal (1973:584-587). In the context of the *ikki*, therefore, the use of millenarian symbols served two purposes. First, it gave religious reinforcement and legitimation to a specific vision of social change as well as the methods used to achieve that vision. Second, the popular symbols of *yonaoshi* and the *Miroku-no-yo* were capable, as we saw in the example of the *eejanaika*, of inspiring powerful expectations and motivations. These in turn stimulated action aimed at achieving the goals set forth by the *ikki* leaders.

In spite of the important differences in the form and content of the nineteenth century millenarian phenomena cited above, there is a common thread which runs through them all. This is the explicit connection made between social protest and utopian aspirations, a connection expressed, furthermore, through millenarian symbols and ideas. As I argued above, millenarian movements are fundamentally revolutionary efforts to break out of oppression. It should be recalled in this context that the socioeconomic conditions characteristic of late nineteenth century Japan described in Chapter II closely match those associated here with the occurrence of millenarian movements. Thus, it is not surprising to find millenarian ideas and symbols in the world views of groups desiring social change, for, as a conceptual mode for apprehending reality and legitimizing social protest, the millenarian paradigm was ideally suited to the experience and concerns of the lower classes in nineteenth century Japan.

It is against this background of popular resistance and utopian aspirations that Nao's appropriation of millenarian ideas and symbols must be seen. She, too, uses the language of the Miroku cult to express her belief in the imminent advent of the millennium: "The time has come for Miroku Bosatsu to enter the world of men and it shall then become peaceful" (5/25/1898; Hino, 1974:23). Moreover, she often refers to the divine kingdom Ushitora-no-Konjin would establish on earth as the *Miroku-no-yo*. One also finds in Nao's *Ofudesaki* frequent references to the age of *Mappō*. This popular Buddhist notion of the "Latter Days of the Law" conformed to her belief that the world had fallen into a totally degenerate and evil state. The direct association Nao makes between the end of *Mappō* and the advent of the *Miroku-no-yo* has deep roots in the folk religious tradition. Finally, as Miyata has pointed out, her emphasis on the reconstruction of the world embodies the idea of *yonaoshi* or world renewal (1975:235). In both content and form, therefore, Nao's world view draws on the popular tradition of millenarian symbols and aspirations. Yet, in Nao's thought, the millenarian paradigm is carried to a much higher level of development and articulation. Unlike the leaders of the other social and religious movements I have discussed, she pursued all its logical implications and left no dimension unexplored. In particular, the image Nao constructed of the ideal world to be established on earth had far more specificity than the images projected by these other movements. She also placed a much greater emphasis on the imminent destruction of the world and its reconstruction by a specific deity. Finally, as I discussed in Chapter II, she introduced a variety of rituals and religious practices (the *shusshu*) which were explicitly intended to bring about the transformation of this world into an ideal one. In accounting for the radical millenarian character of Nao's thought and cult, Yasumaru Yoshio emphasizes her abject poverty and exclusion from the almost miraculous military, cultural and economic success of the Meiji state. He suggests that Nao's extreme eschatological and utopian ideas can only be understood as the expression of her profound resentment of a modernizing (and increasingly capitalistic) society (1977:173).

Yasumaru's explanation echoes Hobsbawm's analysis of European millenarian movements. Nao's millenarian cult, like the movements Hobsbawm studied, was established in a situation where capitalism had recently irrupted into peasant society and people were subjected to pervasive government control. As I pointed out earlier, the economic and social reforms enacted by the Meiji government had negative rather than positive effects for Nao and others like her. Their poverty and social dislocation were exacerbated, not alleviated, by the Meiji land reforms, system of taxation, and industrialization policies. At the same time, through the passage of a universal conscription law in 1873, the establishment of compulsory education (including state control of the curriculum) in the 1880s, the unification and expansion of a national police force, and the institution of licensing procedures for all religious organizations, the Meiji government was able to make its presence felt in almost every sphere of public and private life. Nao's response to this profound socioeconomic change and loss of autonomy, like that of Hobsbawm's revolutionaries, was to reject it and those who furthered it as totally evil. Proclaiming the imminent end of this degenerate society, Nao constructed her own vision of the sacred community she believed must soon replace it -- a vision in direct conflict with that of the Meiji state.

As in all millenarian movements, it is this rejection of secular forms of authority in favor of the divine authority of a specific deity (Ushitora-no-Konjin) which gives Nao's world view its politically subversive character. Yet, paradoxically, implicit in her notion of the ideal community is the desire to ultimately eliminate politics. We see this in Nao's insistence that a shared faith in and obedience to *kami*, not economic relations (money) or political relations (government force) should be what binds people together. In Nao's view, all people were the children of *kami* and thus equal before him. She believed that everyone should be given an even chance in life so that there would be no partiality in people's fortunes. Nao's call for a leveling of society reflects her condemnation of the present social order in which the interests of the majority were subordinated to the greater (and thus unjust) power of a small political and economic elite. Here, too, with her stress on the horizontal rather than vertical relations characteristic of human association, Nao's thinking follows the millenarian paradigm. Privileging religion over politics, she envisioned a sacred community of morally upright individuals living in peace, equality, and mutual respect under the benevolent rule of Ushitora-no-Konjin.

The focus of our attention so far has been the sociopolitical dimension of Nao's vision of reality. I would like to turn now to an analysis of the cognitive and moral dimensions of her world view. Here, too, the millenarian paradigm provided the basic framework in terms of which she integrated selected folk religious beliefs and practices into her teachings and resolved her primary concerns. Once again, the millenarian paradigm together with Shinto notions of purity and pollution will be identified as the sources of the coherence we find in Nao's thought and the ritual practices of her cult.

Purity and Order

There is an unfortunate tendency among historians of Japanese religion to underestimate the importance of the cognitive or conceptual dimension of the new religions. Although there are some, like Reiyūkai Kyōdan in which the founders made a conscious decision to avoid any detailed explanations of their doctrine, preferring instead to focus on religious experience and simple reverence for the Lotus Sutra (Hardacre, 1983:25,31), this should not be seen as a general characteristic of all the new religions. One source of the failure to give adequate consideration to this dimension seems to be the incorrect identification often made between the terms "intellectual" and "conceptual," but the absence of (or even an aversion to) an intellectual approach in no way precludes the existence of a conceptual dimension. As I indicated in the previous discussion of millenarianism, "conceptual" or "cognitive" refers to the efforts made by the leaders of such movements or sects to reformulate their basic assumptions about what is real or true and to construct a new system of values and categories to account for their experience of oppression in a rapidly changing society. In the case of Ōmotokyō, both Nao and Onisaburō were deeply concerned with the problem of explicating their doctrines and produced voluminous religious tracts intended to illuminate the general as well as immediate implications of their teachings. Although Nao (unlike Onisaburō) took an explicit anti-intellectual stance, she still succeeded in formulating a new system of classification, a detailed cosmology, a complex system of religious symbols and concepts, and even a simple epistemology. The following analysis of the conceptual dimension of Nao's millenarian world view begins with a brief discussion of her theory of knowledge and then proceeds to a more extensive examination of the cosmological and symbolic components of her thought.

Nao's notion of what constitutes legitimate knowledge rests primarily on her own experience of divine revelation, for she believed that the only true knowledge was that which came directly from Ushitora-no-Konjin. Her *Ofudesaki*, the record of his revelations, was thus the only legitimate source of truth in the present world: "these scriptures shall hold true forever and shall be written down, as mankind cannot see (the truth) without them" (9/30/1898; Hino, 1974:26). The "truth," of course, was that Ushitora-no-Konjin was going to reconstruct the presently evil world into a new divine realm. According to Nao, however, "people nowadays are all simply deaf and blind" to the truth -- they do not see the world as it really is (1/1892; Hino, 1974:2). Relying on knowledge from "false books," they refuse to listen to the truth and in their ignorance stubbornly persist in their evil and arrogant ways. Concluding that evil spirits had made "this present life dark with worldly learning" (11/26/1915; Hino, 1974:144), Nao completely rejected the legitimacy of secular knowledge (*chie*) and learning (*gaku*). As she asks in her *Ofudesaki*, "Who could possibly understand (Ushitora-no-Konjin's) divine plan through mere worldly cleverness and learning?" (8/10/1900; Hino, 1974:52). Rather, Nao insisted that it was only through faith in Ushitora-no-Konjin's protective power and spiritual reform in accordance with his teachings that true understanding and knowledge could be achieved. Because her *Ofudesaki* is the sole repository of truth in an otherwise dark and evil age, she repeatedly enjoins her followers to read it carefully and fix its teachings in their minds.

Nao's rejection of profane knowledge also includes the doctrines of established religions: with the reconstruction of the world, "the incorrigible mediators of churches" with "their puny doctrines" shall be "judged first" and, one gathers, condemned (1/1899; Hino, 1974:31). Nao's experience of *kamigakari* and her conception of her unique role as Ushitora-no-Konjin's spokesperson convinced her that she was the only legitimate intermediary between the sacred and profane worlds, between the gods and human beings. If Nao was, as she believed, preaching the truth, then everyone else could only be preaching lies. Not surprisingly, in Nao's vision of the ideal society soon to be established on earth, there is no place for traditional religious and educational institutions. Human beings, at one with *kami*, would have no need for religious mediators and, having attained spiritual perfection, would naturally know all that is worth knowing.

As do most religious world views, Nao's includes a cosmological theory of the origin of the universe and its consequent development. Generally speaking, cosmologies serve to demonstrate the ways in which supernatural forces influence the course of events in the phenomenal world and, by ascribing to human beings a specific place in the cosmos, define their relationship to the sacred. The understanding that a divine agent has been involved in the creation of the universe is used to show that it has a purpose, an ultimate destiny. In this way, cosmologies integrate the present with a view of the past and a vision of the future. They not only explain, therefore, the power and intention of supernatural forces, but also provide a system of classification or world view which enables people to order their experience and act meaningfully in terms of a cosmic vision of what is real or significant and what is not.

In elaborating her initial message of world reconstruction, Nao developed a detailed cosmology to account for the degeneration of the world into its present evil and chaotic state. The principal actor in this drama is Ushitora-no-Konjin, the *kami* who first possessed her. This deity (also known as Kimon-no-Konjin) was the evil guardian of the northeast direction ("Ushitora," or "cow-tiger," signifies this direction in Taoist cosmologies) whose "curse of the seven deaths" was widely feared. Shugendō specialists popularized this deity in their rituals of divination and appeasement commonly associated with travel and construction, activities which often required orientation or movement toward the northeast and thus the possibility of offending Ushitora-no-Konjin. Kawate Bunjirō, the founder of Konkōkyō, despite his observance of the necessary precautions, was a victim of the "curse of the seven deaths" before his own possession by Ushitora-no-Konjin. Following his experience of *kamigakari*, however, Bunjirō became convinced that Ushitora-no-Konjin was in fact a good rather than evil *kami* who had created the world and now served as its divine protector (Hori, 1968:233-235).

Nao, as we know, was exposed to Konkōkyō beliefs both before and after her own possession experience. Although her doctrine of the imminent reconstruction of the world differed significantly from Konkōkyō's emphasis on the pursuit of happiness in this world through spiritual reform, Nao did share Bunjirō's reassessment of Ushitora-no-Konjin's true character. According to Yasumaru Yoshio, this transformation of a formerly evil *kami* into a benevolent one was a common feature of Japanese folk religion (1977:128). This was because the notion of *kami* (spirits or gods) was an inherently ambivalent and often amoral one in Japanese folk belief and thus open to a variety of interpretations.

Whether the actions of a particular *kami* were seen as destructive or beneficial depended on one's point of view and the circumstances surrounding its manifestation.

In Nao's view, then, Ushitora-no-Konjin was the creator of the universe, the divine protector of humankind, the healer of the sick, the source of all true knowledge, and the ultimate judge of right and wrong, good and evil. After reconstructing the world, this merciful and just *kami* would reign as its supreme ruler. Nao's conception of Ushitora-no-Konjin as a creator and savior deity should not be seen as the result of Christian influences. Although there were groups of *Kakure Kirishitan*[31] in the Ayabe area, Nao's notion of this *kami* has much more in common with the popular belief in *ujigami*, tutelary deities associated with particular villages and neighborhoods. These tutelary deities were worshipped as protector gods who watched over the local inhabitants, guarding them from harm and preserving their general well-being. The relationship between these *kami* and their "flocks" was compared to that which should exist between parents and children -- a relationship of interdependence and mutual care and respect. In her *Ofudesaki*, Nao also speaks of the people as "the children of *kami*" and insists that "*kami* cannot go without the service of the people, even as the people cannot get along without his care: this is where the two must become interdependent" (5/25/1898; Hino, 1974:23). Furthermore, Nao's religious doctrine in no way conforms to Christian monotheism, in spite of the superficial similarities. Rather, Nao affirmed the vast pantheon of spirits and gods in Japanese folk religion and frequently referred to them in her teachings. According to Nao, Ushitora-no-Konjin had been given his mission to manage affairs in the human world and serve as its ruler by Tsukihi-sama, the ruler of Heaven. She thus considered Tsukihi-sama and Amaterasu (the Sun Goddess) to be superior to Ushitora-no-Konjin (Yasumaru, 1977:143).

Nao's cosmology takes as its point of departure Ushitora-no-Konjin's creation of the human world. In the beginning, this world was a pure and ordered one in which the people lived together in peace, harmony and obedience to the will of Ushitora-no-Konjin. It wasn't long, however,

---

[31] *Kakure Kirishitan* (hidden or clandestine Christians) were Christian believers of the Tokugawa period (1600-1868) who survived the government's prohibition edict of 1614 and succeeding suppressions by going underground. These hidden communities of Christians continued to practice their faith in secret and, without priests or printed manuscripts, orally transmitted their teachings and prayers from generation to generation. In 1873, when the prohibition edicts were finally abolished, more than 30,000 *Kakure Kirishitan* emerged from isolation.

before a group of evil *kami* usurped the rule of the world and forced Ushitora-no-Konjin into exile in the northeast corner. These evil *kami* assumed the titles of good *kami* and declared that Ushitora-no-Konjin was actually an evil god. This is said to have occurred three thousand years ago (Yasumaru, 1977:129). Since that time, the world has been dominated by evil *kami* and for this reason has degenerated from its originally pure and ordered state into the present chaotic world of "beasts" where "good and evil are reversed." Under the influence of these evil *kami*, people have "neglected" the true divine ruler and the world has become an "utterly dark" place (4/10/1903; Hino, 1974:121).

Nao suggests that Ushitora-no-Konjin was overthrown because he overestimated his own strength and righteousness and thus disobeyed the rules of Heaven (Yasumaru, 1977:130). While trying to establish order and justice in the world, he selfishly failed to consider the welfare and feelings of human beings and other *kami*. The incredible hardships he suffered after his fall from power transformed him, however, from a merely correct *kami* to one filled with love and compassion for others (Yasumaru, 1977:133). Just as Nao believed that her own suffering had prepared her for her divine mission, so too Ushitora-no-Konjin's suffering prepared him for his mission to save humankind from total destruction. Thus, although in exile, Ushitora-no-Konjin did not forget his "children": "Like the cuckoo in Japan whose voice is audible but its (figure) invisible, Ushitora-no-Konjin has been protecting you from behind the scenes" (5/1/1903; Hino, 1974:121). "While evil has flourished," he has been "helping the world from the unseen" (8/5/1900; Hino, 1974:44). By Nao's time, however, the situation had deteriorated to the point where the world was on the brink of total destruction, so "unseen protection (was) no longer so useful" (5/1/1903; Hino, 1974:121). Thus, Ushitora-no-Konjin finally manifested himself through Deguchi Nao to reveal his true character to the people and save the world. Because he had been pushed out of the world, it was Nao's mission to put him back into it (Yasumaru, 1977:140).

Far from overlooking the logical implications of this cosmological scheme, Nao articulated them quite clearly. If the world is entirely evil, then the only sacred place left on earth must be Ayabe, the place where the truly good *kami*, Ushitora-no-Konjin, manifested himself through Nao. Even Amaterasu, contrary to popular belief, no longer resides in Ise, but has returned to Heaven to escape earthly defilement (Yasumaru, 1977:196). Although Nao identified several other sacred places through the *shusshu*, Ayabe remained the central reference point in this process of geographical and symbolic sacralization.

As streams and brooks babbling down valleys never fail
to join a greater river till at last they are united into one,
so is this place (Ayabe) the pivot where the true *kami*
resides (1/1892; Hino, 1974:3).

In this sense, Nao's conception of Ayabe fits Mircea Eliade's
notion of the sacred center. His argument that a hierophany, or
manifestation of the sacred, reveals a fixed axis for all future orientation,
both temporal and spatial (1957:21), certainly holds true in this case.
Ayabe, the place where Nao directly experienced contact with the sacred,
the place where the sacred was made manifest through her *kamigakari*, is
the sacred center in a profane world and the physical link between this
otherwise evil world and the new (good) one to be established. Thus, it is
the "source" of *kami's* plan to reconstruct the present world as well as the
place from where the gods will rule over a new divine kingdom in the
future.

At this point in Nao's thought, however, one is struck by an
important transposition. "Ōmoto," the term which refers to Nao's teachings
about the true *kami* (and later, of course, to the religion she founded) is
identified with this sacred place: both are the "great source" (*ōmoto*) or
"great origin" (also read *ōmoto*) of the new world soon to be established.
A story related in the Seventy-Year History of *Ōmoto* (*Ōmoto nanajūnen-
shi*, Vol. I:84) suggests the derivation of this identification. Some time
after Nao's experience of *kamigakari* and acceptance of her divine mission,
her daughter Hisa came to visit her. Nao took Hisa into the backyard of
her home and said to her, "Here, in this garden, is the ancient residence of
kami. Here I will build a shrine for Ushitora-no-Konjin, the *kami* of the
earth. Because this sacred place has become the great source of the world,
I have planted *ōmoto*" (an herb of the lily family).

In her conceptualization of Ōmoto's primary function as the "great
source" of the world, Nao did not stop with these clever plays on words,
but further developed the idea in terms of two metaphors or symbols which
appear again and again in the *Ofudesaki*, the "bridge" and the "mirror":

(Ushitora-no-Konjin's plan) is just like building stone
bridges for crossing to and fro, or iron ones, strong
enough not to give way: this Ōmoto of Ushitora-no-
Konjin is the great bridge of the world (8/8/1900; Hino,
1974:49).

Ōmoto shall be the mirror of the world and what shall
occur on earth shall previously occur here to be

observed... It means that this place shall be the source for making the world which is pitch dark into a crystal clear one (8/20/1900; Hino, 1974:60).

As a "bridge," Ōmoto enables human beings to pass from a state of absolute evil to one of absolute good; to move, that is, from this world into the next. At the same time it serves as a "mirror" which does not simply reflect the present, but, more like a crystal ball, enables one to see into the future: Ōmoto "is the base where examples of future world events are shown" (5/10/1902; Hino, 1974:96); it is the place where "the fundamental actions for becoming crystal clear must be shown" (10/19/1902; Hino, 1974:114). Ōmoto, in other words, is both the "place where everything is made known to the world" (5/22/1902; Hino, 1974:99) and the "absolute foundation for world salvation" (5/10/1902; Hino, 1974:97).

Consistent with her identification of Ōmoto with Ayabe, Nao thus conceives of Ōmoto's role in the world in concrete, spatial terms. The *Ofudesaki* repeatedly encourages people "to come to Ayabe" or "to come to Ōmoto" to hear the truth and participate in *kami's* plan to reconstruct the world. It seems that one must be physically present in Ayabe or Ōmoto to cross the "bridge" or to look into the "mirror." In her overall cosmological scheme, therefore, Nao assigns to Ōmoto the necessary function of mediating between the present and the future, chaos and order, evil and good.

The cosmological scheme I have outlined above is diagrammed in Figure 1 (page 95). The reader will immediately recognize in this diagram the millenarian paradigm. Except for the specific roles assigned to Ushitora-no-Konjin and Ōmoto, it could easily serve as a representation of any fundamentally millenarian world view. At the same time, however, the diagram shows that Nao's vision of reality was also structured and articulated in terms of folk Shinto notions of purity and pollution, order and chaos. These two conceptual modes are not, of course, antithetical, but may be used to reinforce one another. As Mary Douglas has pointed out, "a strong millennial tendency is implicit in the way of thinking of any people whose metaphysics push evil out of the world of reality" (1966:171). Conversely, the idiom of purity and pollution is easily incorporated into millennial visions, for the quest for purity, like that for an earthly utopia, is pursued through rejection: "purity is hard and fast, the enemy of change, of ambiguity, of compromise" (Douglas, 1966:162). Thus, Nao's affirmation of the new world to come as a perfectly ordered, good and pure state of existence logically rests on her rejection of the present world as a completely chaotic, evil and polluted place. However, even though Nao's world view includes much of the language and structure of folk Shinto notions of purity and pollution, it also differs in significant ways from this mode of apprehending the world. As we shall see, in appropriating this belief system within the dominant framework of the millenarian paradigm, Nao transformed many of its implicit meanings and assumptions.

Mary Douglas has written extensively about world views dominated by purity and pollution beliefs, for they are a distinguishing feature of many of the world's religions. Douglas argues that "the search for purity is an attempt to force experience into logical categories of non-contradiction" (1966:162). It is a search for wholeness, perfection, and order. Beliefs about purity and pollution enable the members of a given culture or religion to maintain their classificatory system and protect it from the threat of anomalous, ambiguous, or foreign events. Such beliefs are thus representative of a particular cognitive mode for distinguishing, separating, and categorizing phenomena. They provide a way to impose order on chaos; a way to order and evaluate social and personal experience.

Within such a world view, the creation of the world assumes primary significance as the first, and so archetypical, transformation of chaos into order. Unfortunately, this original order is difficult to maintain because social and biological processes are inherently polluting. Accordingly, humans must periodically perform rituals of purification to restore the world to its originally pure and ordered state. This is doubly important because communication and unification with the sacred is only possible in the pure state -- pollution cuts society off from divine sources of power and protection. Purification rites are thus often seen as a ritual re-enactment of the creation of the world and time is perceived as a continuous oscillation between the ordered state of the world as it existed at the moment of creation and the chaotic, polluted state into which it periodically degenerates (see Leach, 1961).

Nao clearly employed this particular conceptual framework in formulating her vision of reality, for she shares with folk Shinto (and other world views dominated by purity and pollution beliefs) certain fundamental assumptions and organizing principles. As the diagram of her cosmological scheme illustrates, Nao divides the world into two opposing categories: good, which is identified with order, and evil, which is identified with chaos. All experience and phenomena are explained and assigned moral value through placement in one or the other of these categories. Although the two should ideally be kept separate, the latter tends to encroach upon

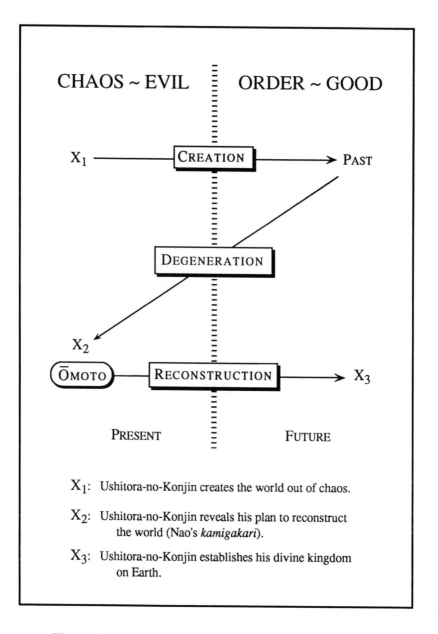

Figure 1. *Diagram of Nao's Cosmological Scheme.*

and thus undermine the former. In her *Ofudesaki*, Nao consistently employs the language of purity and pollution to characterize these two categories or (as she sees them) states of existence. For Nao, that which is ordered and good is "right-side up," "unified," "crystal clear," "light," and pure. That which is chaotic and evil is "upside down," "divided," "clouded," "dark," and polluted. Furthermore, Nao assumes that perfect order and absolute purity are attainable (if not in this world, then in the new world to come) by human beings through spiritual reform, prescribed rituals and divine assistance. In fact, unification with the (legitimate) divine sources of power and protection is only possible within such a pure and ordered state. It is for this reason that Nao views Ōmoto (and thus Ayabe) as an oasis of order, goodness and truth in an otherwise moral and social wasteland -- the "source," therefore, of unification with the sacred. Finally, Nao emphasizes the creation of the world as the archetypal transformation of chaos into order. In her teachings, the "reconstruction" of the world represents a transformation running parallel to and at times even re-enacting the creation. Both are processes in which order is established out of chaos.

The term Nao used to refer to the "reconstruction" was *tatekae-tatenaoshi*.[32] Her conception of this term has much in common with the idea of *yonaoshi* so popular in nineteenth century Japan. *Tatekae* is the nominal form of the transitive verb *tatekaeru*, which means "to rebuild or to reconstruct." *Tatenaoshi* is the nominal form of the transitive verb *tatenaosu*. It also means "to rebuild, to remodel, or to reconstruct," but has other more specific connotations as well: "to restore something to its former state" or "to tear down an old house or other building and construct it anew." It is no mere coincidence that *tatekae* and *tatenaoshi* are common construction terms. Both Nao's grandfather and her husband were carpenters, so she was no doubt familiar with them. From Nao's perspective, the world was really like a dilapidated old house whose beams had rotted through -- before it collapsed in on itself it had to be demolished and a new world built in its place. With their connotations of degeneration, destruction, and reconstruction, the terms *tatekae* and *tatenaoshi* enabled Nao to metaphorically represent and more powerfully communicate her

---

[32] According to Yasumaru Yoshio (1977:210), Nao originally used only *tatekae* and later, under Onisaburō's influence, added *tatenaoshi*. From Nao's point of view, the latter word served to specify more concretely, and thus reinforce, the meaning of the former. During the Taishō period, however, Onisaburō assigned two different meanings to the words, identifying *tatekae* with the destruction of the present world and *tatenaoshi* with its reconstruction. Because the *Ofudesaki* was transcribed by Onisaburō, both words are used in the early as well as late entries. Although I have used both words in this paper to refer to the "reconstruction," I have interpreted them from Nao's, not Onisaburō's, point of view.

notion of the imminent transformation of the world. As it says in the *Ofudesaki*, because the world "can no longer stand as it is, *kami* has manifested himself to carry out the *tatekae-tatenaoshi*" (1/1892; Kozawa, 1973:158).

Although Nao's notion of the *tatekae-tatenaoshi* clearly implies both the destruction (end) of the present world and the establishment (beginning) of the new world, she developed this notion far beyond the explicit meaning of these terms. Because it is a transformation of chaos into order, she also described it as a process of "reversal," one which will turn this "upside-down" world "right-side up." In addition, she often speaks of it as the "restoration" of this world to its originally ordered state, to the way it was when Ushitora-no-Konjin first created it. Finally, consistent with her identification of "ordering" with "purifying," Nao frequently refers to the *tatekae-tatenaoshi* as a process of purification, employing the typically Shinto metaphor for purity of cleanliness: the reconstruction is compared to "a great cleansing (*ōsōji*) and great laundering (*ōsentaku*) of the three thousand worlds" (1/1892; Kozawa, 1973:158). In this respect, the *tatekae-tatenaoshi* is the ultimate rite of purification. Conducted on a cosmic scale, it will result in a new sacred order from which all evil will be eliminated; a "crystal clear" world in which "things shall...never be out of order on any occasion" (8/4/1900; Hino, 1974:44). Like the creation of the world, but in contrast to its gradual degeneration, the *tatekae-tatenaoshi* will be accomplished instantaneously.

Nao's emphasis on the *tatekae-tatenaoshi* and the divine utopia it will create has important consequences for her perception of the past and the passage of time. In this respect, her thinking follows assumptions implicit in the millenarian paradigm rather than those characteristic of folk Shinto. As I indicated earlier, the passage of time in a world view like that of folk Shinto is perceived as an infinite number of oscillations between the two opposing states of purity and pollution, order and chaos. In Nao's world view, however, as the diagram of her cosmological scheme shows, this infinite number of oscillations is reduced to three: the creation of the world (chaos to order), the degeneration of the world (order to chaos), and the reconstruction of the world (chaos to order). Rather than viewing the passage of time as an endless series of alternations between two opposing states, Nao instead viewed it as a linear succession of transformative processes resulting in one state or the other. From her perspective, the passage of time since the creation appears as a unilinear descent into chaos.

Although Nao empties the past of positive value, she does not deny its objective reality. Indeed, it is this negative conception of the past which enables her to account for the present evil state of the world. In this respect, Nao's mode of apprehending the past is distinctly historicist. Whereas historicist thought in the west has tended, however, to view the past as a single movement forward ("progress") toward a more humane and civilized present, Nao viewed it as a continuous process of moral decline: things had gotten worse, not better, since the creation of the world. Moreover, in Nao's conception of the past, historical events as we would define them lose their specificity. Subsumed under an undifferentiated process of degeneration, such events are meaningful only as examples of the increasingly evil and chaotic state of the world. It is because her conception of history is essentially a mythological one that such "human" events are of such little importance to Nao. The principal actors in her historical narrative are gods (Ushitora-no-Konjin and the *kami* who overthrew him), not human beings. And the only significant event or "turning point" (as she calls it) in this history of degeneration is not, for example, the Meiji Restoration (as some of her contemporaries might have argued), but her own *kamigakari* -- the moment when Ushitora-no-Konjin finally manifested himself to reveal the truth about the world and his plan to reconstruct it. The mythological history which Nao develops through her cosmological scheme is thus a central component of her vision of reality, for it enables her to locate herself and her followers in cosmic as well as social time and space.

However, even as Nao uses a historicist mode to link the present to a specific past, she also envisions a future in which there will be no history. Utopian visions embody, after all, a desire for eternal peace and happiness: implicit in the desire to establish the perfect society, a society which will never change, is the desire to abolish history. Paradoxically, then, millenarian world views invent "an anti-historical principle of superior moral force enjoining the destruction of the past/present" to legitimize innovation or radical change (Hobsbawm, 1972:4). Nao's revelation of Ushitora-no-Konjin's plan to establish a new sacred order on earth thus enabled her to both articulate and legitimize her desire for a radical break with the past/present. As she wrote in her *Ofudesaki*, "This world will be changed completely into a new world...a divine realm which will last for all eternity" (1/1892; Kozawa, 1973:158).

The influence of the millenarian paradigm on Nao's thought was not limited, however, to her conception of history and her cosmology. It was also central to her construction of a system of symbols which enabled her to more powerfully communicate her vision of reality to her followers. In appropriating a variety of symbols and metaphors from everyday life within the framework of her millenarian aspirations, Nao infused them with new meaning and significance. As we saw in the case of Nao's reinterpretation of Ushitora-no-Konjin's true character, this transformative process was primarily one of inversion: Nao took ideas, objects or symbols which were negatively valued in Japanese folk culture and gave them a positive meaning or, vice versa, employed traditionally positive ideas, objects or symbols to represent that which she believed to be evil or wrong. The following examples will illustrate how this conceptual mode of symbolic inversion functioned in Nao's thought.

I will begin with a very simple example. It is written in the *Ofudesaki* that "Hitherto, North has been called evil, but North shall be good, for it is the origin of the new world" (7/5/1898; Hino, 1974:24). It will be recalled that "north," the direction commonly associated with bad luck in Japanese folk belief, is also the direction associated with Ushitora-no-Konjin, the direction in which he was exiled and from which he re-entered the world to carry out the reconstruction. In keeping with her reinterpretation of Ushitora-no-Konjin, Nao inverts the popular understanding of this direction, thereby reinforcing her assertion that people are no longer able to distinguish between good and evil.

The following story provides a more complex example of Nao's use of symbolic inversion. Shortly after Nao's first *kamigakari*, her daughter Hisa came to visit her. Hisa tried to give her mother a gift of money, but Nao refused to take it and instead offered Hisa a lump of dirt, saying "There is life because there is soil. You do not understand how much more important a single lump of dirt is than all the money in the world. Money is the source of the world's destruction" (*Ōmoto nanajūnen-shi*, Vol. I, 1964:84). Here, Nao places the highest value on that which is commonly thought to be worth nothing -- dirt. Money, however, is identified with the selfish, materialistic society Nao has rejected. The fact that most people completely disregard the value of dirt/soil (the source of human life), but view the accumulation of wealth as a positive value to be pursued wholeheartedly serves to reinforce Nao's belief that the world has degenerated into a totally evil state. In Nao's teachings, "money" comes to symbolize all that is wrong with the present society.

Nao even employed the logic of symbolic inversion to explain her own life and her new role as Ushitora-no-Konjin's divine spokesperson. Within the prevailing social order, Nao had no more value than a lump of dirt. As a penniless, uneducated widow, she was of no use to anyone and unworthy of social respect. Yet, it was Nao who had been chosen to assist Ushitora-no-Konjin in his efforts to save the world. To Nao, this contradiction was proof that people were so defiled by evil they could no longer recognize what was of value and what was not. Just as the true value of dirt was not recognized, so too Nao's real value and the importance of her special mission were not appreciated.

The central role played by this mode of symbolic inversion in Nao's thinking derives for the most part, therefore, from her rejection of the present society as one in which everything is "topsy-turvy" or "upside-down": that which appears to be good is actually evil and that which appears to be evil is in reality good. It is this inverted perception of the world which led Nao to favor what were commonly thought to be inconsequential or negative things and to devalue those commonly viewed as important or positive. As Mary Douglas has suggested, "If a people takes a symbol that originally meant one thing and twisting it to mean something else, energetically holds on to that subverted symbol, its meaning for their personal life must be very profound" (1970:60). In Nao's case, her creation of new symbols of good and evil through a logical process of inversion was inspired by her millennial aspirations and directly tied to her efforts to represent a vision of a new world radically different from the present one. At the same time, however, Nao's use of symbolic inversion also derives from her classification of all experience and phenomena into the two opposing categories of good and evil. In this respect, her inversion of conventional symbols and metaphors enabled her to further articulate and reinforce not only her criticism of the present and her utopian vision of the future, but also the basic system of classification underlying her world view. Thus, as a conceptual mode of transformation, symbolic inversion (and subversion) can facilitate the communication of both a millenarian world view and one like folk Shinto which represents good and evil in terms of purity and pollution beliefs.

Clifford Geertz (1973:91-92) has argued that a symbol "is any object, act, event, quality, or relation which serves as a vehicle for conception; the conception is the symbol's meaning." Symbols are thus the "concrete embodiments of ideas, attitudes, judgements, longings or beliefs." As "extrinsic sources of information, they provide a blueprint or template in terms of which processes external to themselves can be given a definite form." In constructing and articulating her vision of reality, Nao employed a wide range of symbols and metaphors from Japanese folk culture and religion. These enabled her to translate an initially personal vision into one which was meaningful to others as well, for through these symbols and metaphors Nao's followers were able to grasp not only the essence, but the broader implications of her religious world view. As in any religious system, however, these symbols fulfilled more than just an explanatory or communicative function. They also served as reference points to structure experience, engendered appropriate emotional states, and inspired correct belief and behavior. We have already encountered many of the symbols and metaphors Nao used in her teachings. Here, therefore, I shall focus briefly on a set of three interrelated symbols which appear often in her *Ofudesaki*: the plum blossom, the cherry blossom, and the pine tree.

In her first entry in the *Ofudesaki*, Nao predicted the *tatekae-tatenaoshi*: "The three thousand worlds shall burst forth all at once, as the plum blossoms do, and be made into the world of Ushitora-no-Konjin" (1/1892; Kozawa, 1973:158). Here, as elsewhere in her writings, the blossoming of the plum tree serves as a metaphor of the *tatekae-tatenaoshi*. In Japan, however, the plum tree not only "bursts into full bloom all at once," it also blossoms very early in the spring when the weather is cold and, quite often, there is still snow on the ground. Thus, the plum blossom is a symbol of the *tatekae-tatenaoshi* not only because it would occur, like the blossoming of the plum tree, instantaneously, but also because the plum blossom is associated with hardship and suffering: "The plum blossom suffers with the cold. Its suffering is long, but sufferings are blessed in this age. Without them, what can you know?" (10/5/1902; Hino, 1974:113). Nao believed that the reconstruction of the world would occur only after people had endured great suffering and hardship. Like the plum blossom, then, the *tatekae-tatenaoshi* would begin in harsh and difficult times. Through the symbol of the plum blossom, Nao was thus able to convey her conception of the reconstruction in more concrete terms. Because the plum blossoms appeared every spring, even in bad weather, this symbol also served to reinforce belief in both the possibility and imminence of the *tatekae-tatenaoshi*. Furthermore, in that it symbolized endurance and the positive value of suffering, the plum blossom provided a source of inspiration for Nao's followers: just as its suffering further enhanced the appreciation of its beauty, their suffering would enable them to realize the truth about the world and achieve the spiritual purity demanded by Ushitora-no-Konjin.

In contrast to the plum blossom, the cherry blossom blooms in late spring when the weather is warm and sunny. Whereas Nao associated the plum blossom with suffering and endurance, she associated the cherry blossom with death and impermanence. "Blossoming without hardships endures only a short while, like cherry blossoms. Splendid as they are at first, they only fall soon" (10/5/1902; Hino, 1974:113). The cherry blossom thus serves as a symbol of the present world, which, like the cherry blossom, cannot last long. "It has hitherto been the age of vain flowers...a wrong age which will not prosper long" (11/30/1898; Hino, 1974:28). The cherry blossom also symbolizes the way of life characteristic of the present world, a way of life Nao condemned: "An easy-going manner of living is one without labor -- that manner is, as it were, like that of the cherry blossom, beautiful to see but without fruit... Without many pains, there can be no harvest" (11/30/1898; Hino, 1974:29). Here, Nao not only affirms the value of a life of labor, but further suggests that without suffering and hard work the reconstruction of the world will not be accomplished. In Nao's symbolic system, therefore, the cherry blossom stands in direct opposition to the plum blossom. The former symbolizes those qualities she rejects and the latter symbolizes those qualities she affirms. It is no wonder, then, that Nao encouraged her followers to "know the comparison between the plum blossom and the cherry blossom" (10/5/1902; Hino, 1974:113), for these symbols expressed what were correct attitudes and modes of behavior in Nao's eyes and what were not.

Whereas the cherry blossom is a symbol of the present world, the new world to come is symbolized by the pine tree (*matsu*). Just as the pine tree is forever green, so Ushitora-no-Konjin's divine realm will last forever. This new world will, moreover, be "ruled by the pine" (*matsu de osameru*) -- an age, in other words, of peace and harmony. Nao's vision of a paradise on earth has many names, but one she uses often is "*matsu-no-yo*," "the world of pines." According to the *Ofudesaki*, "The world of pines, which has been longed for since ancient times, is coming..." (11/30/1898; Miyata, 1975:247). In this context, the phrase "*matsu-no-yo*" takes on a double meaning, for *matsu* can mean either "pine tree" or "to wait". Thus, the *matsu-no-yo* is both the "world which will last forever," like the pine that is always green, and the "much awaited world," the age of peace and happiness "longed for since ancient times." The symbol of the pine tree serves, therefore, as both a concrete representation of Nao's vision of a divine utopia and as an expression of her millennial yearnings. But Nao not only associates the pine tree with patience, peace and immutability. She also associates it with strength, endurance and moral constancy. In this respect, the pine tree is used to symbolize qualities similar to those identified with the plum blossom, for it, too, prospers in harsh environments: growing in sandy soil or clinging to rocky cliffs, it retains its color throughout the long, cold winter. Nao accordingly enjoined her followers "to be of firm purpose" and serve *kami* "with an unmovable will like that of the pine." Like the plum blossom, then, the pine tree is a symbol which can inspire correct behavior and attitudes. "The pine is always green, constant in color; *kami's* heart is immutable, but the human heart is changeable... The heart of (*kami*) is the color of pine needles: have only the heart of the pine and you will be able to endure forever" (12/3/1901; Hino, 1974:85).

In appropriating and developing these three symbols within the framework of her millenarian vision of reality, Nao infused them with new meaning and significance. In particular, following the process of symbolic inversion I discussed above, she subverted the generally positive value attributed to the cherry blossom in Japan. Rather than the symbol of that which is unique or valuable in Japanese culture, in Nao's teachings it becomes a symbol of the society she has rejected. The plum blossom and the pine tree are instead elevated as symbols of what is to be positively valued and aspired to. Taken together, these three symbols form a coherent system of inter-related and mutually reinforcing ideas, attitudes and judgements that are meaningful not only at a cosmic level, but also have immediate implications for individual belief and action. It was through the formulation of symbols like these that Nao was able to communicate her new vision of reality to her followers and to steer their thought and behavior in directions she believed appropriate.

In the discussion thus far of the central message of Nao's teachings as well as the cosmological and symbolic components of her world view, frequent reference has been made to her concern with morality and spiritual reform. Like that of all millenarian movements and sects, Nao's world view has an important moral dimension. In Chapter II, I showed how her deep commitment to the *tsūzoku dōtoku* provided a reference point for her radical critique of the prevailing social order. In Nao's view, human beings had become worse than "fierce beasts" with no other purpose in life than to fulfill their basest desires. They attached too much importance to money and had no compassion or respect for others. They were selfish, conceited and avaricious. They were, in fact, so defiled and confused by evil that good things looked bad to them and wrong acts appeared right (7/11/1902; Hino, 1974:103).

Nao did not stop, however, at merely condemning people's evil minds and degenerate behavior. Deeply troubled by what she perceived as a general acceptance of this rampant immorality, she also developed a system of values and moral virtues to serve as a guide for conduct in accordance with her vision of the ideal human community. Rejecting material wealth, worldly learning and political power as determinants of social status, she instead held up this moral code as the only true measure of human worth and social prestige, the only valid source of personal integrity and religious salvation. Like the *tsūzoku dōtoku* from which it is in part drawn, this moral code encourages frugality, diligence and self-discipline and posits loyalty, obedience, filial piety, and sincerity (*makoto*) as the most noble of human virtues. To these moral prescriptions implicit in the *tsūzoku dōtoku*, Nao added faith in Ushitora-no-Konjin, obedience to his will and gratitude for his protection. She also encouraged her followers to be humble and polite in all situations and to help others in distress. Reminding them that "*Kami* dislikes quarrels, lamentations and complaints" (1896; Hino, 1974:11), she urged them to live cheerfully in peace and harmony with one another. Finally, she enjoined them to conquer their selfish desires and false pride so that they might better serve Ushitora-no-Konjin.

Nao's insistence that her followers reform their spirits through behavior in conformance with this moral code derives in part from her belief that spiritual reform was the only possible route to salvation and admission to the new world to come. She also believed, however, that Ushitora-no-Konjin would not carry out the *tatekae-tatenaoshi* until as many people as possible had reformed themselves, for those who did not would perish in the destruction of the present world. Nao usually refers to this point in accounting for her "failures of prophecy." According to Nao, the compassionate Ushitora-no-Konjin postponed the *tatekae-tatenaoshi* in the hope that more people would be able to reform themselves and thus be saved. In Nao's view, then, the achievement of a paradise on earth depended on human effort as well as divine power. This is reflected not only in the urgent tone of the *Ofudesaki*, but also in the importance Nao attributed to the *shusshu*. In order to insure that the *tatekae-tatenaoshi* would occur in the immediate future, she and her followers had to work hard to spread the teachings of Ushitora-no-Konjin and reform themselves in accordance with those teachings.

In Nao's world view, therefore, spiritual reform is believed to have soteriological consequences for both the individual and the world. This dual function is symbolically reinforced by the notions of purity and pollution which, along with the *tsūzoku dōtoku*, inform Nao's conception of morality and spiritual reform. She repeatedly instructs her followers not only to act in accordance with her moral code, but also to "purify" their hearts and minds and "polish" the clouded mirrors of their spirits. Moral defects are, in other words, a kind of pollution: although evil may "darken" the human spirit, like pollution it can be "removed" or "washed away" through rituals of purification. In this respect, Nao affirms the traditional Shinto belief in the original purity of the human spirit. Humans are not the source of evil (rather it invades them from the outside) nor are they burdened with either a fundamentally or permanently evil nature. At the same time, however, they are required to take responsibility for evil by acting to rid themselves of it and return their spirits to their originally pure state. Although Nao thus acknowledges the objective reality of evil, she ultimately denies its inevitability in her conviction that an absolute state of purity and goodness is possible. As previously noted, this particular understanding of evil also underlies her belief in the degeneration and imminent reconstruction of the world. It should be recalled in this context that Nao even describes the *tatekae-tatenaoshi* as a great cleansing or purification of the world. Within the framework, therefore, of her purity and pollution beliefs, the human spirit comes to represent a microcosm of the larger world. The purification of the former is thus both structurally homologous to, and symbolic of, the purification of the latter. From this perspective, spiritual reform not only facilitates the *tatekae-tatenaoshi*, it also represents it in the concrete experience of the individual. Because both are processes of purification, they share the same goals: to eliminate all evil and to achieve union with the sacred, whether it be in this world or the new one to come.

This emphasis on purification in Nao's world view is also characteristic of the *shusshu*. In that these ritualized missions were intended to induce the *tatekae-tatenaoshi*, all contributed in one way or another to the ultimate purification of the world. Moreover, as in the pilgrimages to Oshima and Meshima, each *shusshu* included ascetic practices like *mizugori* (cold water ablutions) intended to purify the spirits of the individual participants. The three *shusshu* Nao conducted in 1901 constitute the most concrete manifestation of her purification beliefs, for the immediate as well as ultimate objective of these missions was the purification of the world.

In the spring of that year, Nao revealed in her *Ofudesaki* Ushitora-no-Konjin's command that she take some of the "crystal pure" water from the spring at Moto-Ise and bring it back to Ayabe. According to Shinto tradition, Moto-Ise is the site of the cave where the Sun Goddess, Amaterasu, upset by the wild behavior of her younger brother, Susanoo-no-Mikoto, hid herself, thereby plunging the world into total darkness. Contrary to popular belief, Nao believed that Amaterasu had never left her hiding place and for this reason, the world was still shrouded in darkness. Before the Grand Shrine of Ise was established in the seventh century, Amaterasu was enshrined at Moto-Ise, hence its name, "Original Ise." On April 26th, Nao travelled to Moto-Ise, a good day's walk to the northwest of Ayabe, with Onisaburō, Sumi, and thirty-nine followers. Although drawing water from the spring at the shrine was forbidden, one of Nao's followers managed to sneak past the priest guarding the shrine precincts and collect some of the sacred water. The next day, after praying at the shrine, the group returned to Ayabe, carrying the precious water in two segments of bamboo. The water was first presented to Ushitora-no-Konjin in a ceremonial offering conducted before his altar. One container was then set aside and the other was passed around so that each person could take a sip. The remaining water was poured into the Ōmoto well.

That same month, Nao received another command from Ushitora-no-Konjin. This time, she was instructed to go to the Grand Shrine of Izumo. The deity enshrined at Izumo is Susanoo's descendant, Ōkuninushi-no-Mikoto who, according to Shinto mythology, ceded control of Japan to the descendants of Amaterasu, reserving for his own line the right to govern the unseen world of gods and spirits. In July, Nao, Onisaburō, Sumi, and twelve followers made the long journey to Izumo. Traveling on foot and by boat, it took them eleven days to reach their destination. There, they prayed at the shrine and received the sacred fire (said to have been kept alight since the age of the gods) as well as some earth from the shrine precincts and some water from the well. After returning to Ayabe, they scattered the earth in places associated with Nao's experience of *kamigakari* and kept the flame burning for one hundred days. They mixed the water with that remaining from Moto-Ise and poured it into the well. Later that month, Nao, accompanied by thirty-five followers, once again travelled to the island of Meshima. From the summit of the rock where they had first landed on the island the previous year, she poured water collected from this well into the sea. As she did so, Nao prayed,

> Oh, Ushitora-no-Konjin, we humbly beseech you, with your power, wide as the Pacific Ocean and deep as the Sea of Japan, to make this pure water from Moto-Ise and Izumo circle the seas of the world, turning to clouds, turning to rain, snow and hail, watering the five continents, cleansing corrupt spirits, washing away impurities, and building a paradise on earth.[33]

In creating the *shusshu*, as in the construction of her world view, Nao appropriated traditional folk religious beliefs and practices within the framework of the millenarian paradigm and Shinto notions of purity and pollution, thereby investing them with new meaning relevant to her own

---

[33] This quotation, as well as my account of the Moto-Ise and Izumo *shusshu*, is taken from a translation of the *Kaiso den* (a biography of Deguchi Nao written by Sakae Ōishi) which appeared in the Ōmotokyō journal, *Oomoto International*, January-March, 1982:32-38.

concerns and aspirations. Although the *shusshu* consist of conventional religious practices such as pilgrimage and rites of purification, these practices do not serve to affirm religious orthodoxies, but rather express and reinforce Nao's heterodox, millennial vision. Through the performance of the *shusshu*, Nao defined religious action in accordance with her world view by demonstrating its content and purpose. In this way, the *shusshu* served as models both for what Nao wanted her followers to believe and how those beliefs were to be put into practice.

But the *shusshu* also spoke to, and inspired, Nao herself: fully one third of the *Ofudesaki* was written between the years 1900 and 1903, the period during which most of the *shusshu* were conducted. In the millenarian cult Nao established, as in all religions, the relationship between belief and ritual, thought and action, was a dialectical one. Nao's world view certainly informed her understanding of religious action and her creation of specific rites, but at the same time, the *shusshu* clarified and validated that world view (articulated it, as it were, in action) and stimulated the moods and motivations she expected of her followers.

IV
Conclusion: Women and Gender
in the New Religions

The picture that finally emerges of Nao's life prior to her *kamigakari* is one of endless toil and hardship -- a life she herself often described as "a cauldron burning in the fires of hell."[34] Against this background of ever-deepening poverty and personal loss, Nao's self-discipline and perseverance are indeed remarkable. Yet, according to Nao's "philosophy of life," a philosophy grounded in the *tsūzoku dōtoku*, this was the way she was supposed to behave. Nao believed that if a woman was loyal and sincere, worked diligently, and endured suffering without complaint, then she would one day acquire the social respect, happiness, and prosperity that her self-abnegation and moral virtue deserved (Yasumaru, 1977:70). It was, therefore, Nao's strict adherence to the ethical code prescribed by the *tsūzoku dōtoku*, and her firm belief in the system of social and moral justice that it implied, that gave her the strength and hope to persevere.

The *tsūzoku dōtoku* thus constituted a powerful ideology of gender in nineteenth century Japanese society, reinforcing partriarchal social and cultural institutions as well as the feminine ideal of the silently suffering, self-sacrificing wife and mother. Meiji leaders later appropriated and institutionalized this gender ideology, giving it a central place in their policies of social control and public education. If we are to fully understand the women who founded new religions, we must examine their experience and consciousness in the context of this pervasive pattern of female subordination, martyrdom, and exclusion from the public sphere of thought and action. In the course of this book, I have tried to show how Nao's socioeconomic status in a rapidly changing society influenced her

---

[34] *"Ah, jigoku no kama no shōkishi to wa ware no koto ka"* (quoted in Yasumaru, 1977:133).

primary concerns and aspirations. Here, I will discuss how gender influenced the form and content of her opposition to prevailing social and religious institutions and ideologies. Unfortunately, scholars have generally ignored gender in their analyses of the new religions, leaving a crucial gap in our knowledge and understanding of this important historical and religious phenomenon.[35] The following discussion is thus intended as a tentative effort to begin filling this gap -- an admittedly incomplete analysis of a very complex problem, but one which should at least demonstrate the central importance of gender in the new religions and suggest possible directions for further research.

In Japan, the view implicit in the *tsūzoku dōtoku* that suffering was an intrinsic part of what it meant to be a woman was reinforced by popular notions of karma. According to the Buddhist doctrine of *henjōnanshi*, it was virtually impossible for women to attain enlightenment or salvation because their bad karma was so much greater than that of men. If women, therefore, were ever to escape the eternal karmic cycle of suffering and rebirth, they must first be reborn as men.[36] The assumption here is that the lives of women are qualitatively different from, and unequivocally worse than, the lives of men -- misery, hardship, and suffering are a woman's inescapable fate. Together, then, the systems of conventional morality and popular religious belief projected an extremely negative and circumscribed vision of female possibilities and virtue. The Meiji woman who wished to preserve her self-respect, achieve public approbation and insure her ultimate salvation had no alternative but to sacrifice her own happiness and endure her suffering with nobility and fortitude. That she often pursued her martyrdom with alacrity further demonstrates the power of this feminine ideal to determine a woman's view of her proper role in the established order.

This ideal of female martyrdom is compellingly illustrated in two contemporary Japanese novels, *The Waiting Years* and *The Doctor's Wife*, which chronicle the tragic lives of two women -- the former fictional, the latter historical. As Gail Lee Bernstein has argued, the characterizations of the female protagonists in these books are in complete conformity with "the Meiji view that women were expected to suffer silently and beautifully"

---

[35] Two scholars of Japanese religion whose work is sensitive to issues of women and gender are Helen Hardacre and Nakamura Kyoko. See the Bibliography for their relevant publications in English.

[36] For a more detailed discussion of the Buddhist doctrine of *henjōnanshi*, see Hardacre, "Gender and the Millennium in Ōmoto Kyōdan," pp. 218-220.

(1980:358). The lives of these women powerfully attest to the fact that the fate of a woman was by definition an unhappy one. Throughout a lifetime of exploitation and emotional deprivation, the two heroines maintain their virtuous silence and fully embrace their roles as devoted, self-sacrificing wives. Their only complaint is that their devotion and self-sacrifice are not appreciated (Bernstein, 1980:356). In their proud acceptance of their unhappy circumstances, these women elevate suffering to a virtue and thus stand as typical examples of the ideal Japanese woman who is "noble in her martyrdom" (Bernstein, 1980:357).

Nao, as the author of her own life story, constructed an identical self-characterization, casting herself in the role of the "noble martyr," a righteous woman who accepted her suffering with silent fortitude. In agreeing to marry Deguchi Masagorō, for example, Nao consciously sacrificed her own hopes and desires. After her husband's death more than thirty years later, she declared that she had always felt that her first love, the young man whom her sense of duty and fear of spiritual retribution forced her to abandon, was her soul's "true husband -- Masagorō merely fathered my children."[37] Yet, in spite of her own unhappiness, she was loyal to Masagorō throughout their marriage. She worked diligently to compensate for his indolence and even shamed herself before her family and neighbors by begging them for the expensive food and liquor he requested from his sickbed. This image of Nao as the self-sacrificing wife and mother, the noble martyr, persists throughout her memoirs. It seems that in her experience of *kamigakari* Nao finally found a context in which she could legitimately break the rule of virtuous silence and voice the misery of her past. It is angry pride, however, not self-pity, that underlies Nao's reflections on a lifetime of hardship, for she, like the heroines above, elevated suffering to a virtue and believed that her self-abnegation was proof of her moral integrity. In her *Ofudesaki*, Nao firmly established the depth of her suffering and the nobility of her martyrdom.

Nao's actions, her moral values, and her self-perception were thus grounded in the popular ideal of female martyrdom. As the primary framework for explaining female experience, however, this social and religious vision of a woman's lot in life ultimately failed to provide her with a satisfactory understanding of her own suffering. How was she to explain, for instance, her failure to achieve the happiness, the prosperity, or even the respect that her perfect compliance with the female role prescribed by the

---

[37] *"Giemon ga honto no mitama no otto de, Masagorō wa tanetori de atta"* (quoted in Yasumaru, 1977:29).

tsūzoku dōtoku should have guaranteed? Was her suffering truly without purpose? As we noted earlier, it was precisely this compulsion to affirm her self-worth and discover the meaning of her suffering that in large part triggered Nao's *kamigakari*. Through this experience of divine possession and revelation she was finally able to determine the reason for her suffering and the significance of her martyrdom.

In an argument that rests on the tautological assumptions implicit in the popular notions of karma discussed above, Nao attributed her hardship and misery to the bad karma she had accumulated in her former lives. The *Ofudesaki* states that her "sin (meguri)[38] was even heavier than the weight of her body" (quoted in Yasumaru, 1977:134). Furthermore, she connected the heaviness of her sin and the depth of her suffering with the fact that she was a woman: although it was commonly believed that a woman's life was more difficult than that of a man because of her greater inherent sinfulness, it was also believed that women were better able than men to endure hardship and suffering. The *Ofudesaki* asserts, therefore, that it was precisely because Nao was a woman, with the powers of resignation and perseverance characteristic of her sex, that she was able to endure the innumerable hardships and intense suffering required by her divine mission. In other words, although it was Nao's fate to suffer, her martyrdom ultimately constituted the preparation for her role as a divine medium. Moreover, Nao's hardships were not only the source of her own redemption, but also enabled her to help others reform and attain salvation. Nao wrote in the *Ofudesaki* that her suffering would enable others to understand the truth: "Nao has suffered for such a long time that now even the flesh has disappeared from her body, but she has suffered for the sake of Ushitora-no-Konjin's great plan to reconstruct the world" (quoted in Yasumaru, 1977:215).

Nao did not stop, however, with this positive re-evaluation of her own suffering and typically female virtues of endurance and perseverance. She also described herself as assertive, resolute, and strict, personality attributes generally associated with men, not women. In fact, Nao insisted that she embodied both male and female characteristics. The term she chose to represent this unique concept of gender duality is *henjōnanshi*

---

[38] *Meguri*, the Japanese reading of zaigō (sin), is here synonymous with karma or fate, *shukumei*. Nao used it to refer to those negative characteristics which the individual had accumulated in past lives. Nao believed that one's *meguri* was the cause of hardship and suffering in one's present existence but she also believed that *meguri* could be overcome (and suffering ultimately eliminated) through spiritual reform, good deeds, and prayer.

Deguchi Nao

(Transformed Male): female in body (sex), but male in spirit or nature (gender). She identified her co-founder, Onisaburō, as her opposite, *henjōnyoshi* (Transformed Female): male in body (sex), but female in nature (gender). Nao often criticized Onisaburō for his strong male ego, but at the same time acknowledged that he was more tolerant, nuturing, and forgiving than she was. In her *Ofudesaki*, Nao skillfully marshalls these complementary concepts to establish and legitimize her own religious authority. On the one hand, being physically female, she was able to endure the profound suffering that was a necessary preparation for her important religious role as Ushitora-no-Konjin's preeminent spokesperson: her mission was such "a great undertaking that it could not be accomplished by those with male bodies" (quoted in Yasumaru, 1977:136). On the other hand, being "male" in nature, Nao was able to articulate and implement a radical message of world renewal which was uncompromising in its harsh demands for moral reform and the eradication of all evil.

Nao's notion of *henjōnanshi* represents a radical departure from the Buddhist theory of *henjōnanshi* (the two terms are pronounced the same but written differently) and a direct challenge to the ideologies of gender which underpin the *tsūzoku dōtoku*. Although Nao shared the premise that men and women are different, at the same time she firmly rejected the negative view of women (or femaleness) central to both Buddhist doctrine and the *tsūzoku dōtoku*. By asserting the positive value of female suffering and creating a model of gender complementarity rather than hierarchy and opposition, Nao was able to assure women of access to salvation in this life. Whereas Buddhist doctrine stressed the negative quality of suffering as a punishment for past evil deeds and the *tsūzoku dōtoku* implied that suffering, as a virtue, was an end in itself, Nao constructed a far more optimistic and purposeful theory of suffering. In her view, suffering constituted both a context for moral reform and spiritual purification and a necessary qualification for those who would serve Ushitora-no-Konjin. Through this reinterpretation of suffering as a legitimate mode of religious austerity or ascetic practice which could enable individuals, both male and female, to attain salvation in this life, Nao transformed what was thought to be a unique characteristic of female experience into a general human one; what was merely a way of life into a religious way of life. By sanctifying hard work, self-sacrifice, and poverty, Nao thus gave suffering a new meaning and a more positive value while at the same time allowing women equal and immediate access to salvation: for Nao, the crucial determinant was an individual's spiritual, not biological, condition.

Although Nao relied heavily on stereotypical male and female traits in her theory of gender transformation, she realligned, reinterpreted, and re-evaluated these traits to create a new, composite vision of the ideal human being -- one who tries to personify the best while striving to eliminate the worst (through suffering) of both genders. It is in this sense that the Transformed Male (Nao) and the Transformed Female (Onisaburō) could stand as models for their followers, both men and women, to admire and emulate as they struggled to put Nao's teachings into practice. Moreover, as Helen Hardacre argues in her fascinating article, "Gender and the Millennium in Ōmoto Kyōdan," Nao's concept of gender transformation is directly linked to her belief in the imminent reconstruction of the world, for only through the parallel efforts of Nao and Onisaburō to acquire and manifest the positive qualities of the opposite gender could Ushitora-no-Konjin's divine realm be established on earth (1992:223). For Nao, then, gender transformation and the suffering that makes it possible were the source of both individual and world salvation.

Nao's resolution of the problem of suffering is central to her religious doctrine. It is used to account not only for her own special role, but to explain Ushitora-no-Konjin's transformation from a malevolent to a benevolent *kami* and to demonstrate the innate evil of the present social order. It is, moreover, an essential element of Nao's general theory of human and divine justice which supports her ideas of world reconstruction and universal salvation. The fact that both Nao's concern with the problem of suffering and her resolution of it were grounded in her experience and consciousness as a woman in a culture where female martyrdom was normative demonstrates the critical importance of gender to an understanding of the new religions -- both the circumstances of their establishment and organizational structure as well as the form and import of their doctrines and rituals.

In this respect, the lives of the female founders of new religions follow a remarkably similar pattern. Like Nao, they subscribed to the conventional ideal of female martyrdom, enduring hardship and suffering with nobility and fortitude. Yasumaru has argued that if these women had lived in more favorable socioeconomic circumstances, they would not have been motivated to found new religions. In other words, if they had received the rewards of prosperity and social respect that their martyrdom should have guaranteed, they would not have perceived the contradiction between their expectations and the reality of their own lives which gave them a vantage point from which to critique the established social order. For Yasumaru, the determining factor is the degree to which their experience alienated them from, rather than integrated them into, society (Yasumaru, 1977:8). There must have been many women, however, whose unrewarded martyrdom alienated them from society but who were never moved to construct a revolutionary vision of reality. Therefore, the experience of martyrdom and alienation, although a central factor in the world views the founders eventually developed, does not alone explain why a woman would devote herself to the establishment of a new religious movement.

The founders did differ from their fellow sufferers, however, in that they hoped to resolve the meaninglessness of their martyrdom. These were self-confident, angry women who never questioned the legitimacy of their own virtue, but rather the legitimacy of a social order that neither acknowledged nor valued their virtue. Strongly committed to the moral code and system of justice implicit in the *tsūzoku dōtoku*, they had definite ideas about the way human beings and society should be. They were critical of the present social order and believed that something better was possible. It is, therefore, less the experience of martyrdom itself than the particular consciousness of that experience that is important.

Like most Meiji women, however, the founders faced quite formidable cultural and legal obstacles in their efforts to communicate their ideas to a wider audience. Although they might hold positions of relative power within their families and work outside their homes, women were precluded by their sex from playing principal roles in the public sphere. The prevailing ideology of gender roles embedded in the cultural norms of the ruling elite and enforced by the Meiji state consigned them to positions of social subservience, political subordination, and silence. Even those self-styled forerunners of enlightened thought and advocates of "women's rights," the intellectuals of the Meiji Six Society, could envision no other roles for women than those of "good wives and wise mothers." In an article published in the society's journal, the *Meiroku Zasshi*, in 1875, Nakamura Masanao demanded equal education for women. His argument was based, however, on his assumption that a woman's proper place was in the home: women must be well educated so that they might better perform their natural vocation as the primary educators of their children. This article, appropriately enough, was entitled "Creating Good Mothers."[39]

---

[39] See Sievers, "Feminist Criticism in Japanese Politics in the 1880s," for a more general discussion of the views on women's rights held by the members of the Meirokusha. Translations of the members' articles on this subject, including Nakamura's, are available in Braisted, *Meiroku Zasshi, Journal of the Japanese Enlightenment.*

There were some Meiji women, of course, who defied convention and broke through the ideological and institutional barriers intended to exclude them from intellectual discourse and political action. The young Higuchi Ichiyō, for example, published a number of short stories in the 1890s which received the highest popular and critical acclaim. In her stories, Ichiyō wrote eloquently and compassionately about the urban poor, the pains of growing up, and the tragically circumscribed lives of Meiji women. As a "woman" writer, however, Ichiyō was commonly regarded as a curiosity -- an assessment which never failed to infuriate her (Danly, 1981:154).[40] There was also Kishida Toshiko, a feminist in the popular rights movement who was "one of the most effective public speakers of her day" (Sievers, 1981:605). From 1882 to 1884, under the official sponsorship of the Liberal Party, she travelled throughout Japan, lecturing on women's rights. In October, 1883, however, following a speech in Osaka, she was jailed and fined for her radical criticism of Japanese social norms and institutions. "Although she continued to lecture in the early months of 1884, the confused condition of the popular rights movement and her own reticence in the face of continued police harassment brought an end to her public speaking career in that year" (Sievers, 1981: 612-613).

In his book, *Reflections on the Way to the Gallows: Rebel Women in Prewar Japan*, Mikiso Hane translates the autobiographical writings of twelve courageous women who actively participated in the struggle to extend human rights to women and minorities and to ensure social justice and economic well-being for everyone. Like Deguchi Nao, they were deeply committed to a new vision of human community and endured great hardships in their efforts to challenge the status quo and transform their society. Unfortunately, the Meiji ruling elite did not share their vision. One of the last acts of the outgoing government in July, 1890, was to revise the already stringent laws on public meetings by adding women to the list of persons denied the right to participate in politics on any level. "Since little else was modified, this addition seems a clear sign of the government's plan to silence the voices of women who had become such outspoken critics of Japanese society and to stifle their potential to generate the social and political change that those in power feared" (Sievers, 1981:615). In the succeeding decade, members of the National Diet refused to change this law

---

[40] Robert L. Danly's (1981) biography of Higuchi Ichiyō (1872-1896) includes translations of nine of her stories. In these stories, Ichiyō denounces the rampant materialism of contemporary society and champions the need for more humanistic values. Like Deguchi Nao, she addressed the problems of social groups excluded from the dominant discourse: women, children, and the poor.

on the grounds that political participation "would ruin the morals of the nation's women" (Sievers, 1981:616). In 1898, the ideological and legal exclusion of women from the public sphere was given further sanction with the promulgation of the new Civil Code. This Code, following the repressive samurai model of the Tokugawa period, denied women any individual rights by subordinating them to the authority of the male head of the household and confined them to circumscribed roles within the domestic sphere.

Against this background of state control and repression, the ability of the founders to break into the public sphere of discourse and action, even though they lacked the educational and social advantages of women like Higuchi Ichiyō and Kishida Toshiko, seems quite remarkable. Folk religion, however, was one sphere of activity outside the domestic realm in which peasant women regularly participated.[41] In fact, women often served as specialists in folk religious practices and cults. One reason for this lies in the particular character and structure of Japanese folk religion: because it straddles the private and public spheres, it tends to blur the distinctions between them. Thus, through their participation in folk religion, women were allowed access to the public sphere and, as mediums and faith healers, often held positions of religious authority in their communities. As was discussed in Chapter I, once the women founders of the new religions had gained access to the public sphere in traditionally sanctioned roles, they were able to transform these roles through the politicization of their religious messages and the creation of new forms of group association. Only later, when they grew more outspoken in their social criticism and began to attract larger numbers of followers (and thus the attention of the authorities as well), were they subjected to police harassment and government suppression. By that time, however, the founders had already established their public identities and articulated their political and religious views.

Although participation in folk religious practices allowed women limited access to the public sphere of discourse and action, it was a woman's experience of *kamigakari* which ultimately enabled her to break out of the prevailing ideology of gender roles and create a new identity for herself. In this respect, the experience of an altered state of consciousness was an inherently liberating one: freed from the categories, values, and

---

[41] It is interesting to note in this context that although women participated in religious forms of popular resistance like the *okage mairi* and *eejanaika*, they were excluded from the peasant uprisings of the eighteenth and nineteenth centuries which were not explicitly religious.

expectations which had formerly determined their thinking and evaluation of the world, the founders suddenly found themselves outside the established system of ideological and social dominance. From this new vantage point, they were able to criticize the established order and construct a vision of reality based on their own experiences and concerns rather than those of a ruling (we might add male) elite. Because this vision therefore included what had been excluded and expressed what had been repressed, it was necessarily in conflict with prevailing ideologies of social order.

This liberating experience was not one, however, that the founders necessarily shared with either their followers or their descendants. Although Deguchi Nao was able to enter the public sphere, the female heirs to her spiritual authority have once again been relegated to the private sphere. Ever since Nao's prophecies failed in 1905, positions of doctrinal and organizational leadership within Ōmotokyō have been occupied by men. Today, Nao's female descendants, although highly esteemed by Ōmoto members, live fairly secluded lives, devoting themselves to the pursuit of various traditional art and literary forms. Their public appearances are limited to (often silent) participation in major rites and festivals, art exhibits, and dramatic performances. They are also called upon to entertain important visitors, but are not supposed to speak out on doctrinal issues or interfere in organizational matters. This restriction of women to the private sphere, which in Ōmoto is identified with spiritual and artistic activity, contrasts sharply with the freedom granted men to participate in either or both the public and private spheres. In fact, those men who evidence administrative skills together with spiritual power and artistic talents are the most respected members of the group.

It is apparent, therefore, that Nao's more radical views, which dissolved the distinction between public and private (thereby transcending the exclusion of women from the former) and politicized a religious vision of the world, have been eliminated from contemporary doctrine. Except for their participation in the international ecumenical and peace movements, Ōmoto leaders eschew any involvement in politics per se -- in Ōmoto "public" action and discourse means religious, not political, action and discourse. This is in part a reaction to the severe government suppression of Ōmoto in the 1920s and 1930s. It is also the result, however, of the leaders' assumption that a commitment to religion (and thus "culture") and to a religious vision of the future obviates the need for politics. In an article on the position of women in the new religions, Nakamura Kyoko (1980) points out that in spite of the initial presence of strong female leadership, the new religions quickly revert to patterns of male dominance and never question the legitimacy of traditional gender roles, but implicitly and explicitly support them. This failure to challenge the prevailing ideology of gender and the social institutions that perpetuate it is the necessary result of a world view in which politics is displaced by culture: in the new religions, the sociopolitical reality of gender asymmetry is denied by reducing the subordination of women in Japanese society to a cultural norm which is considered natural or given. We must conclude, therefore, that soteriological equality for women (a hallmark achievement of the new religions) was seen as an end in itself, neither requiring nor inspiring the social and political equality one might otherwise associate with it.

For the founders themselves, however, the experience of an altered state of consciousness clearly had a liberating effect. In addition to freeing her from ideological constraints, *kamigakari* provided a woman with a unique outlet for her creative energies at a time when few such opportunities existed for women of low social status and limited education. Although rarely considered in this light, the establishment of a new religion was in fact a highly creative endeavor. In their efforts to construct and articulate a new world view and persuade others of its relevance and truthfulness, the founders became prolific writers of doctrinal treatises, social commentaries, sermons, autobiographical accounts, and poetry. They also introduced new forms of group association and worship and created new rituals in conformity with their religious doctrines. The founders were intelligent, reflective, imaginative individuals who, through their experience of an altered state of consciousness, were able to actualize and direct their creative potential.

As I argued in Chapter I, *kamigakari* is an essentially cognitive experience (one of knowing more than feeling) and is thus best understood as a creative process rather than a psychological aberration. In his analysis of cognition and creativity, Lawrence S. Kubie has posited the existence of a "preconscious intellect which, by making free use of analogy and allegory, and superimposing dissimilar ingredients into new perceptual and conceptual patterns," enables the individual to achieve "that fantastic degree of condensation without which creativity in any field of activity would be impossible" (1961:34-35). In trance, as in the creative process and even dreams, the workings of this preconscious intellect are permitted to come into consciousness (Greeley, 1974:53-54), thus providing the individual with the otherwise inaccessible knowledge and inspiration necessary for the construction of a new world view. Like most shamans, the founders, through their experience of an altered state of consciousness, acquired heightened powers of interpretation, synthesis, and insight and became adept at imposing order on chaos and assigning meaning to the inexplicable.[42]

In Japan, however, where spirit possession is a culturally acknowledged phenomenon, the eruption of the "preconscious intellect" into consciousness is often experienced as possession by an outside power. Because this altered state of consciousness is so radically different from the individual's normal state, it is identified not with her own will or thought, but with those of a separate spiritual entity which has "entered" her body. The founders thus claimed to be speaking and acting not for themselves, but for the powerful deities who had possessed them. They accordingly believed that their religious doctrines were the product of the god's infinite and divine wisdom rather than the result of their own creative efforts. It is interesting that this deity was invariably identified as a male spirit. Consequently, many of the founders, like Nao, spoke in a deep, masculine voice when in a state of trance and in their writing and preaching used a style and tone characteristic of male rather than female spoken language. Kitamura Sayo, the woman who founded Tenshō Kōtai Jingūkyō (more commonly known as the Dancing Religion) even dressed in male clothing.[43]

This practice of male identification is certainly linked, in Nao's case at least, with her theory of gender duality or gender transformation (henjōnanshi). It is an excellent example of how Nao gave meaning to her personal experience through her religious teachings and how that experience in turn was used to validate those teachings and communicate them to her followers in a more concrete way. However, this male identification has other implications which should also be considered. First, to achieve an authoritarian tone, the women founders had little choice but to adopt male speech patterns, for it would be difficult to express the will of a powerful deity in the polite and humble forms characteristic of female language. A recognition of this language problem helps explain Nao's difficulty in verbally asserting the authority of her own religious views because, apart from her experiences of kamigakari and her writing in the Ofudesaki, Nao continued to use the more modest female speech forms which were not conducive to aggressive arguments, stern commands, or harsh criticism.

---

[42] For a further discussion of the modes of cognition and interpretation characteristic of shamans, see Lévi-Strauss, *Structural Anthropology*, pp. 167-206, and Shweder, "Aspects of Cognition in Zinacanteco Shamans."

[43] For a detailed discussion of Kitamura Sayo's life and thought, see Nakamura, "No Women's Liberation; the Heritage of a Woman Prophet in Modern Japan."

Only in a state of trance (*kamigakari*) was Nao able to assert her own point of view and express her anger at those who questioned her authority: the Tenrikyō priests, Okumura, Onisaburō, and her followers.

Second, there is a striking analogy between the founders' claims to speak for a male deity and the use of male pseudonyms by women writers in the West. In both cases, the adoption of a male identity allowed more immediate access to the public sphere of thought and action dominated by men. By conforming to definite cultural assumptions of male social and intellectual superiority, both practices assured a woman of a larger and more sympathetic audience and granted her statements a legitimacy and authority which they might otherwise have been denied.

In this chapter I have tried to show the significance of gender to our analysis and understanding of the new religions. By locating the men and women who established these lay organizations in a specific sociocultural context, we are able to identify the ideologies of gender which informed their experience and consciousness, ideologies which they in turn appropriated, challenged, and transformed. The women founders of new religions did not pursue a feminist agenda, but they did view their own gender as problematic. Deguchi Nao developed her concept of gender transformation specifically to resolve the contradictions she perceived between her biological/social identity as a woman and her role as a religious leader, a role not condoned for women by the social or religious gender ideologies of the time. Furthermore, women's unequal access to salvation was a central concern of all of the founders, regardless of their own gender. Breaking with traditional religious doctrine which held that a woman had first to be reborn as a man to achieve salvation, the founders of the new religions eliminated the gender barrier, declaring that women, like men, could achieve salvation in this life through their own efforts.

A focus on gender illuminates, therefore, the ideological and institutional constraints and possibilities which shaped the personal identity and religious teachings of the individuals who established new religions. These and related issues associated with women and gender in the new religions certainly require further research and analysis, particularly in conjunction with the issue of class. However, based solely on this study of Deguchi Nao and Ōmotokyō, we can conclude that a few remarkable women, through an experience of *kamigakari*, were able to transcend their circumscribed social role and transform themselves into religious leaders and political actors striving to realize a revolutionary vision of human nature and community.

Glossary of Japanese Terms

borokai	ボロ買い	rag collecting
butsudan	仏壇	ancestral shelf
byōki naoshi	病気直し	faith healing
chie	知恵	secular knowledge, wisdom
chinkonkishin	鎮魂寄進	ritualized method of spirit possession, divination, exorcism and meditation
chōnin	町人	townspeople
eejanaika	エージャナイカ	literally, "Why not, it's okay!" or "anything goes"; mass movements of wild dancing and rejoicing which broke out on the eve of the Meiji Restoration (fall and winter of 1867)
Fuji-kō	富士講	devotional association of laymen and women centered on the worship of Mt. Fuji
gaku	学	learning
geta	下駄	wooden platform sandals

henjōnanshi	変成男子	Buddhist doctrine of female salvation which holds that women cannot attain Buddhahood because they have too much bad karma; they must first be reborn as men before they can escape the eternal karmic cycle of suffering and rebirth
henjōnanshi	変性男子	Transformed Male; in Nao's teachings, one who is female in body but male in spirit, like Nao herself, and thus able to achieve salvation in this life
henjōnyoshi	変性女子	Transformed Female; in Nao's teachings, one who is male in body but female in spirit, like Onisaburō, and thus able to achieve salvation in this life
hiragana	平仮名	Japanese phonetic syllabary
hiromae	広前	place for group worship (church), especially in Konkōkyō
hotoke	仏	Buddha, buddhas
hyōrei	憑霊	spirit possession
ie	家	house, household
ikki	一揆	(peasant) uprising
Inari-kō	稲荷講	devotional association focused on the worship of Inari, the tutelary deity of rice cultivation and the five grains
itako	イタコ	blind female medium

Jiyū minken undō	自由民権運動	Movement for Freedom and Popular Rights, a nationwide political movement of the early Meiji period (1868-1912)
Jiyūtō	自由党	Popular Rights Party
kakun	書訓	house rules
kami	神	god, deity
kamidana	神棚	household altar (literally, "god shelf") used to enshrine Shinto deities in the home
kamigakari	神懸かり、神憑	spirit possession
kana	仮名	phonetic script
kanji	漢字	Chinese characters
kannushi	神主	Originally the head priest of a shrine or a person qualified to serve as a medium; Shinto priest
keireki	経歴	personal history
kō	講	popular devotional associations
koku	石	volume measure (180 liters)
Konkōkyō	金根教	new religion founded by Kawate Bunjirō (1814-1883)
makoto	真	sincerity, honesty, truthfulness
manjū	饅頭	steamed bean-jam bun
Mappō	末法	the latter days of the Dharma; the end of time

matsu	松	pine tree
matsu de osameru	松で収める	to rule by the pine tree
matsu-no-yo	松の世 待つの世	the world of pines; the much awaited world
meguri	罪業	sin, karma, fate
miko	巫女	priestess serving as ceremonial assistant at a Shinto shrine; also a female medium
Miroku	弥勒	(Sanscrit: Maitreya, "The Benevolent One") Bodhisattva who, at the end of time, will descend to earth and lead everyone to enlightenment
Miroku odori	弥勒踊り	special dances performed in conjunction with songs announcing the advent of Miroku
Miroku-no-yo	弥勒の世	the world of Miroku; the divine realm he is to create on earth
miwakeru	見分ける	to determine, verify
mizugori	水垢離	cold water ablutions
mochi	餅	rice cake
namazu-e	鯰絵	woodblock prints of catfish
norito	祝	ancient Shinto liturgy or prayer
nyūjō	入定	state of deep meditation or suspended animation
obi	帯	sash, belt

Ōharae norito	大祓祝	ancient Shinto liturgy of purification and spiritual renewal
okage mairi	おかげ参り	"worship to return divine favor"; spontaneous, periodic mass pilgrimages to the Ise Shrines during the Tokugawa period (1600-1868)
ōmoto	万年青	plant of the lily family
ōmoto	大本 大元	great source or foundation; great origin
Ōmotokyō	大本教	new religion founded by Deguchi Nao in 1892
on	恩	favor, benefit, debt of gratitude
ōsentaku	大洗濯	the great laundering
ōsōji	大掃除	the great housecleaning
otoritsugi	御取り次ぎ	ritualized mode of meditation, intended to renew the participant's bond with kami
Reiyūkai Kyōdan	霊友会教団	new religion founded by Kubo Kakutarō, his brother and daughter-in-law, Kotani Kimi, in 1925
saniwa	さ庭	male participant in ritualized spirit possession who determines the identity of the spirit possessing the medium
seisei ka-iku	生成化育	divine way of creation and growth
shinkō chiryō	信仰治療	faith healing

shinkō shūkyō	新興宗教	new religions
shinrei no hyōi	神霊 の 憑依	spirit possession
shintai	神体	object of worship which symbolizes or embodies a particular deity
shirei	死霊	spirits of the recently deceased
Shugendō	修験道	religious order which prescribes ascetic practices in mountains to attain magic powers beneficial to the community
shugyō	修業	ascetic practice; religious training and discipline
shukumei	宿命	karma, fate
shusshu	出修	ritualized activities involving pilgrimages to sacred sites initiated by Deguchi Nao from 1900 to 1905
sorei	祖霊	ancestral spirits
tatekae tatenaoshi	立替建て直し	reconstruction of the world
Tenrikyō	天理教	new religion founded by Nakayama Miki (1798-1887)
tsukimono	憑き物	spirit which has possessed an animate or inanimate object
tsūzoku dōtoku	通俗道徳	conventional morality
ujigami	氏神	tutelary deities of villages or neighborhoods

Ushitora-no-konjin	艮の金神	evil guardian of the Northeast direction; the popular deity who possessed Nao
yamabushi	山伏	male shamans associated with mountain sects, especially Shugendō
yonaoshi	世直し	world renewal
zaigō	罪業	sin

Selected Bibliography

Ackroyd, Joyce
    1959   "Women in Feudal Japan." *Transactions of the Asiatic Society of Japan*, third series, Vol. 7, pp. 31-68.

Ahern, Emily
    1975   "The Power and Pollution of Chinese Women." In *Women in Chinese Society*, Margery Wolf and Roxane Witke, eds. Stanford: Stanford University Press.

Ariyoshi, Sawako
    1978   *The Doctor's Wife*. Tokyo: Kodansha International.

Bellah, Robert N.
    1957   *Tokugawa Religion*. Glencoe, Illinois: The Free Press.

Bernstein, Gail Lee
    1980   "The Model Japanese Woman." *The Journal of Japanese Studies*, Vol. 6, No. 2 (summer).
    1983   *Haruko's World: A Japanese Farm Woman and her Community*. Stanford: Stanford University Press.
    1991   editor, *Recreating Japanese Women, 1600-1945*. Berkeley: University of California.

Berthon, Jean-Pierre
    1985   *Espérance millénariste d'une nouvelle religion japonaise*. Cahiers d'études et de documents sur les religions du Japon, no. 6. Paris: Atelier Alpha Bleu.

Bingham, Marjorie Wall and Susan Gross
    1987   *Women in Japan from Ancient Times to the Present.*
            St. Louis Park, MN: Glenhurst Publications.

Blacker, Carmen
    1971   "Millenarian Aspects of the New Religions in Japan."
            In *Tradition and Modernization in Japanese Culture*,
            Donald H. Shively, ed.   Princeton: Princeton
            University Press.
    1976   *The Catalpa Bow.* London: George Allen and Unwin
            Ltd.

Bourdieu, Pierre
    1977   *Outline of a Theory of Practice.* Cambridge:
            Cambridge University Press. (1972)

Bowen, Roger W.
    1980   *Rebellion and Democracy in Meiji Japan.* Berkeley:
            University of California Press.

Braisted, William R.
    1976   *Meiroku Zasshi, Journal of the Japanese
            Enlightenment.* Cambridge: Harvard University Press.

Burridge, K.O.L.
    1960   *Mambu: A Melanesian Millennium.* New York:
            Humanities Press.
    1969   *New Heaven New Earth.* New York: Schocken Books.

Bynum, Caroline Walker, Steven Harrel, Paula Richman, eds.
    1986   *Gender and Religion: On the Complexity of Symbols.*
            Boston: Beacon Press.

Chambliss, William
    1965   *Chiaraijima Village.* Tucson: University of Arizona
            Press.

Cohn, Norman
    1957   *The Pursuit of the Millennium.* London: Secker and
            Warburg.

Comaroff, Jean
    1985   *Body of Power, Spirit of Resistance: the Culture and History of a South African People.* Chicago: University of Chicago Press.

Danly, Robert Lyons
    1981   *In the Shade of Spring Leaves: The Life and Writings of Higuchi Ichiyō, A Woman of Letters in Meiji Japan.* New Haven: Yale University Press.

Davis, Winston
    1980   *Dojo: Magic and Exorcism in Modern Japan.* Stanford: Stanford University Press.

Deguchi, Nao
    1968   *Ōmoto shinyu* (Five Volumes). Kameoka: Ōmoto.
    1973   *Keireki no shinyu.* Kameoka: Ōmoto Nanajūnenshi Hensankai.
    1977   *Hyō no shinyu.* Kameoka: Ōmoto Kyōgaku Kensanjo.

Deguchi, Sumiko
    1976   *Osanagatari.* Kameoka: Tenseisha (1955).

Douglas, Mary
    1966   *Purity and Danger.* New York: Frederick A. Praeger, Publishers.
    1970   *Natural Symbols.* New York: Vintage Books.
    1972   "Pollution." In *Reader in Comparative Religion: An Anthropological Approach.* W. Lessa and E.Z. Vogt, eds. New York: Harper and Row.

Dye, Nancy Schrom
    1979   "Clio's American Daughters: Male History, Female Reality." In *The Prism of Sex*, J.A. Sherman and E.T. Beck, eds. Madison: University of Wisconsin Press.

Earhart, H. Byron
    1969   "The Interpretation of the New Religions of Japan as Historical Phenomena." *Journal of the American Academy of Religions*, Vol. 37, No. 3 (September), pp. 237-248.

1970   *A Religious Study of the Mt. Haguro Sect of Shugendō.* Tokyo: Sophia University Press.

1980   "Toward a Theory of the Formation of the Japanese New Religions: A Case Study of Gedatsu-kai." *History of Religions*, Vol. 20, Nos. 1-2, pp. 175-197.

1982   *Japanese Religion: Unity and Diversity*, 3rd edition. Belmont, CA: Wadsworth Publishing Company.

1989   *Gedatsu-Kai and Religion in Contemporary Japan: Returning to the Center.* Bloomington and Indianapolis: Indiana University Press.

Eliade, Mircea

1959   *Cosmos and History: The Myth of the Eternal Return.* New York: Harper and Row (1949).

1961   *The Sacred and the Profane.* New York: Harper and Row (1957).

Enchi, Fumiko

1971   *The Waiting Years.* Tokyo: Kodansha International.

Fairbank, John K., E.O. Reischauer, and A.M. Craig

1965   *East Asia: The Modern Transformation.* Boston: Houghton Mifflin Company.

Foard, James H.

1982   "The Boundaries of Compassion: Buddhism and National Tradition in Japanese Pilgrimage." *The Journal of Asian Studies*, Vol. 41, No. 2 (February), pp. 231-251.

Fruin, Mark

1980   "Peasant Migrants in the Economic Development of Nineteenth Century Japan." *Agricultural History*, Vol. 54, No. 2 (April), pp. 261-277.

Fukuzawa, Yukichi

1988   *Fukuzawa Yukichi on Japanese Women.* Translated and edited by Eiichi Kiyooka. Tokyo: University of Tokyo Press.

135

Furuki, Yoshiko
  1991   *The White Plum: A Biography of Ume Tsuda.* New
          York and Tokyo: Weatherhill.

Garon, Sheldon
  1986   "State and Religion in Imperial Japan, 1912-1945."
          Journal of Japanese Studies, Vol. 12, No. 2, pp. 273-
          302.

Geertz, Clifford
  1973   *The Interpretation of Cultures.* New York: Basic
          Books.

Gluck, Carol
  1978   "The People in History: Recent Trends in Japanese
          Historiography." *Journal of Asian Studies*, Vol. 38,
          No. 1 (November), pp. 25-50.
  1985   *Japan's Modern Myths: Ideology in the Late Meiji
          Period.* Princeton: Princeton University Press.

Goldmann, Lucien
  1970   "The Sociology of Literature." In *The Sociology of Art
          and Literature*, Albrecht Barett, ed. New York:
          Praeger.
  1973   "Genetic Structuralism." In *The Sociology of Literature
          and Drama*, Elizabeth and Tom Burns, eds. Penguin
          Books edition.

Greeley, Andrew M.
  1974   *Ecstasy: A Way of Knowing.* Englewood Cliffs:
          Prentice-Hall.

Guthrie, Stewart
  1988   *A Japanese New Religion: Risshōkōseikai in a
          Mountain Hamlet.* Ann Arbor: Center for Japanese
          Studies, University of Michigan.

Hane, Mikiso
  1982   *Peasants, Rebels, and Outcasts: The Underside of
          Modern Japan.* New York: Pantheon.

1988 *Reflections on the Way to the Gallows: Rebel Women in Prewar Japan.* Berkeley: University of California Press.

Hardacre, Helen

1982 "The Transformation of Healing in the Japanese New Religions." *The Journal of the History of Religions*, Vol. 20, No. 3 (May), pp. 305-320.

1983 "The Cave and the Womb World." *Japanese Journal of Religious Studies*, Vol. 10, Nos. 2-3, pp. 149-176.

1984 *Lay Buddhism in Contemporary Japan: Reiyūkai Kyōdan.* Princeton: Princeton University Press.

1986 "Creating Shinto: The Great Promulgation Campaign and the New Religions." *Journal of Japanese Studies*, Vol. 12, No. 1, pp. 29-63.

1986 *Kurozumikyō and the New Religions of Japan.* Princeton: Princeton University Press.

1988 "Gender and the Millennium in Ōmoto Kyōdan: the Limits of Religious Innovation." In *Innovation in Religious Traditions: Essays in the Interpretation of Religious Change*, Michael Williams, Collett Cox, and Martin S. Jaffee, eds. Berlin and New York: Mouton de Gruyter.

1989 *Shinto and the State, 1868 - 1988.* Princeton: Princeton University Press.

Harootunian, Harry D.

1982 "Ideology as Conflict." In *Conflict in Modern Japanese History*, Tetsuo Najita and J. Victor Koschmann, eds. Princeton: Princeton University Press.

1988 *Things Seen and Unseen: Discourse and Ideology in Tokugawa Nativism.* Chicago: University of Chicago Press.

Havens, Thomas R.H.

1974 *Farm and Nation in Modern Japan: Agrarian Nationalism, 1870-1940.* Princeton: Princeton University Press.

Hino, Iwao P., translator

1970   *The Outline of Oomoto.* Kameoka: Ōmotokyō (1958).

1974   *Ofudesaki: The Holy Scriptures of Oomoto* (Excerpts). Kameoka: Ōmotokyō.

Hobsbawm, E.J.

1965   *Primitive Rebels.* New York: W.W. Norton and Company, Inc. (1959).

1972   "The Social Functions of the Past: Some Questions." *Past and Present,* No. 55 (May), pp. 3-17.

Hori, Ichiro

1968   *Folk Religion in Japan.* Joseph M. Kitagawa and Alan L. Miller, eds. Chicago: University of Chicago Press.

Ikeda, Akira, editor

1982   *Ōmoto shiryō shūsei* (Collected Historical Materials on Ōmoto). Tokyo: San'ichi Shobō.

Inglis, Jean, editor and translator

1991   *The Prison Memoirs of a Japanese Woman: Kaneko Fumiko.* Armonk, New York: M.E. Sharpe.

Irokawa, Daikichi

1985   *The Culture of the Meiji Period.* Marius B. Jansen, trans. Princeton: Princeton University Press.

Ishimoto, Shidzue

1984   *Facing Two Ways: The Story of My Life.* Stanford: Stanford University Press (1935).

Jansen, Marius B. and Gilbert Rozman

1986   *Japan in Transition: From Tokugawa to Meiji.* Princeton: Princeton University Press.

Kelly-Gadol, Joan

1976   "The Social Relation of the Sexes: Methodological Implications of Women's History." *Signs* Vol. 1, No. 4 (summer), pp. 809-823.

Kendall, Laurel
    1985   *Shamans, Housewives, and Other Restless Spirits.*
              Honolulu: University of Hawaii Press.

Ketelaar, James E.
    1990   *Of Heretics and Martyrs in Meiji Japan: Buddhism and
              Its Persecution.* Princeton: Princeton University
              Press.

Kidd, Yasue Aoki
    1978   *Women Workers in the Japanese Cotton Mills: 1880-
              1920.* Ithaca: Cornell University East Asia Papers.

Kikumura, Akemi
    1981   *Through Harsh Winters: The Life of a Japanese
              Immigrant Woman.* Novato, CA: Chandler and Sharp.

Kitagawa, Joseph M.
    1966   *Religion in Japanese History.* New York: Columbia
              University Press.
    1981   "The Career of Maitreya, with Special Reference to
              Japan." *History of Religions*, Vol. 21, No. 2
              (November), pp. 107-125.
    1987   *On Understanding Japanese Religion.* Princeton:
              Princeton University Press.

Kondo, Dorinne K.
    1990   *Crafting Selves: Power, Gender, and Discourses of
              Identity in a Japanese Workplace.* Chicago:
              University of Chicago Press.

Kozawa, Hiroshi
    1973   "Utopia shisō." In *Kindai Nihon shūkyō-shi shiryō*
              (Nihonjin no shūkyō, Vol. 4), Tamaru Noriyoshi,
              Muraoka Kū, and Miyata Noboru, eds. Tokyo: Kōsei
              Shuppansha.

Kubie, Lawrence S.
    1961   *Neurotic Distortion of the Creative Process.* New
              York: Noonday Press.

Leach, Edmund R.
>   1961   "Two Essays Concerning the Symbolic Representation
>   of Time." In *Reader in Comparative Religion: An
>   Anthropological Approach*. W.A. Lessa and E.Z.
>   Vogt, eds. New York: Harper and Row.

Lebra, Joyce, Joy Paulson, and Elizabeth Powers, editors
>   1976   *Women in Changing Japan*. Stanford: Stanford
>   University Press.

Lebra, Takie Sugiyama
>   1984   *Japanese Women: Constraint and Fulfillment*.
>   Honolulu: University of Hawaii Press.

Lévi-Strauss, Claude
>   1963   *Structural Anthropology*. New York: Basic Books,
>   Inc.

Marra, Michele
>   1988   "The Development of *Mappō* Thought in Japan (I)."
>   *Japanese Journal of Religious Studies*, Vol. 15, No. 1,
>   pp. 25-54.
>   1988   "The Development of *Mappō* Thought in Japan (II)."
>   *Japanese Journal of Religious Studies*, Vol. 15, No. 4,
>   pp. 287-305.

Matsumae, Takeshi
>   1980   "The Heavenly Rock-Grotto Myth and the *Chinkon*
>   Ceremony." *Asian Folk Studies*, Vol. 39, No. 2, pp.
>   9-22.

McClellan, Edwin
>   1985   *Woman in the Crested Kimono: The Life of Shibue Io
>   and Her Family Drawn from Mori Ōgai's "Shibue
>   Chūsai."* New Haven: Yale University Press.

McFarland, H. Neill
>   1967   *The Rush Hour of the Gods*. New York: Macmillan.

Miyata, Noboru
>   1975   *Miroku shinkō no kenkyū*. Tokyo: Miraisha.

1983 "Various Types of Maitreya Belief in Japan," unpublished manuscript.

Mosk, Carl
 1980 "Nuptiality in Meiji Japan," *Journal of Social History*, Vol. 13, No. 3, pp. 474-489.

Murakami, Shigeyoshi
 1971 "Bakumatsu ishinki no minshū shūkyō ni tsuite." In *Minshū shūkyō no shisō*, Vol. 67 of Nihon shisō taikei. Tokyo: Iwanami Shoten.
 1980 *Japanese Religion in the Modern Century*, H. Byron Earhart, trans. Tokyo: University of Tokyo Press (1968).

Nadolski, Thomas Peter
 1975 "The Socio-Political Background of the 1921 and 1935 Ōmoto Suppressions in Japan." Ph.D. dissertation, University of Pennsylvania.

Najita, Tetsuo
 1970 "Ōshio Heihachirō (1793-1837)." In *Personality in Japanese History*, Craig and Shively, editors. Berkeley: University of California Press.

Nakamura, Kyoko Motomochi
 1980 "No Women's Liberation: The Heritage of a Woman Prophet in Modern Japan." In *Unspoken Worlds*, Nancy A. Falk and Rita M. Gross, eds. San Francisco: Harper and Row.
 1981 "Revelatory Experience in the Female Life Cycle: A Biographical Study of Women Religionists in Modern Japan." *Japanese Journal of Religious Studies*, Vol. 8, Nos. 3/4, pp.187-205.
 1983 editor, *Women and Religion in Japan*, special issue of the *Japanese Journal of Religious Studies*, Vol. 10, Nos. 2/3.

Nolte, Sharon H., and Sally Ann Hastings
    1991   "The Meiji State's Policy Toward Women, 1890-1910."
           In *Recreating Japanese Women, 1600-1945*, Gail Lee
           Bernstein, ed. Berkeley: University of California.

Norman, E. Herbert
    1940   *Japan's Emergence as a Modern State.* New York:
           The Institute of Pacific Relations.

Offner, Clark B. and Henry Van Straelen
    1963   *Modern Japanese Religions.* Tokyo: Rupert Enderle.

Oguchi, Iichi and Takagi Hiroo
    1969   "Religion and Social Development." In *Japanese
           Culture in the Meiji Era*, Vol. II: Religion. Kishimoto
           Hideo, ed. Tokyo: Tōyō Bunko (1956).

Ohkawa, Kazushi, and Henry Rosovsky
    1965   "A Century of Japanese Economic Growth." In *The
           State and Economic Enterprise in Japan.* Princeton:
           Princeton University Press.

Ōmoto Nanajūnen-shi Hensankai
    1964   *Ōmoto nanajūnen-shi*, Vol. I. Kameoka: Ōmotokyō.

Oomoto International
    1956-   English quarterly. Official journal of the Oomoto
           Foundation and the Aizenkai (Universal Love and
           Brotherhood Association). Kameoka-shi, Kyoto-fu 621,
           Japan: The Oomoto Foundation.

Ong, Aihwa
    1987   *Spirits of Resistance and Capitalist Discipline:
           Factory Women in Malaysia.* Albany: State
           University of New York Press.

Ouwehand, Cornelius
    1964   *Namazu-e and Their Themes: An Interpretive Approach
           to Some Aspects of Japanese Folk Religion.* Leiden:
           E.J. Brill.

Pharr, Susan J.
    1981   *Political Women in Japan*. Berkeley and Los Angeles: University of California Press.

Philippi, Donald L. (translator)
    1959   *Norito: A New Translation of the Ancient Japanese Ritual Prayers*. Tokyo: The Institute for Japanese Culture and Classics, Kokugakuin University.

Pocock, J.G.A.
    1973   *Politics, Language and Time*. New York: Atheneum.

Robertson, Jennifer
    1991   "The Shingaku Woman: Straight from the Heart." In *Recreating Japanese Women, 1600-1945*, Gail Lee Bernstein, ed. Berkeley: University of California Press.

Rose, Barbara
    1992   *Tsuda Umeko and Women's Education in Japan*. New Haven: Yale University Press.

Sakurai, Tokutarō
    1974   *Nihon no shamanism*, Vol. I. Tokyo: Yoshikawa Kōbunkan.
    1977   *Nihon no shamanism*, Vol. II. Tokyo: Yoshikawa Kōbunkan.

Satō, Noriaki
    1981   "The Initiation of the Religious Specialists *Kamisan*: a Few Observations." *Japanese Journal of Religious Studies*, Vol. 8, Nos. 3/4, pp. 149-186.

Scheiner, Irwin
    1970   *Christian Converts and Social Protest in Meiji Japan*. Berkeley: University of California Press.
    1973   "The Mindful Peasant: Sketches for a Study of Rebellion," *The Journal of Asian Studies*, Vol. 32, No. 4 (August), pp. 579-591.

Schneider, Delwin B.
    1968   *Konkōkyō*. Tokyo: The International Institute for the Study of Religions (1962).

Scott, Joan Wallach
    1988   *Gender and the Politics of History*. New York: Columbia University Press.

Shambaugh, Cynthia
    1978   "Spirit Possession and Trance: The Relationship Between States of Consciousness and Culture." Unpublished paper presented at the American Anthropological Association, Los Angeles.

Shambaugh, Cynthia & Irving Zaretsky
    1978   *Spirit Possession and Spirit Mediumship in Africa and Afro-America*. New York: Garland Publishing Co.

Shimazono, Susumu
    1979   "The Living *Kami* Idea in the New Religions of Japan." *Japanese Journal of Religious Studies*, Vol. 6, No. 3 (September), pp. 389-412.
    1987   "Spirit-belief in New Religious Movements and Popular Culture: The Case of Japan's New Religions." *The Journal of Oriental Philosophy*, Vol. 26, No. 1, pp. 90-100.

Shweder, Richard A.
    1972   "Aspects of Cognition in Zinacanteco Shamans: Experimental Results." In *Reader in Comparative Religion: An Anthropological Approach*, W.A. Lessa and E.D. Vogt, eds. New York: Harper and Row.

Sievers, Sharon L.
    1981   "Feminist Criticism in Japanese Politics in the 1880s: The Experience of Kishida Toshiko," *Signs*, Vol. 6, No. 4 (summer), pp. 602-616.
    1983   *Flowers in Salt: The Beginnings of Feminist Consciousness in Modern Japan*. Stanford: Stanford University Press.

Smith, Robert J.
    1973   "Town and City in Premodern Japan: Small Families, Small Households, and Residential Instability." *Urban Anthropology*, A. Southall, ed. New York: Oxford University Press.
    1974   *Ancestor Worship in Contemporary Japan*. Stanford: Stanford University Press.
    1987   "Gender Inequality in Contemporary Japan." *Journal of Japanese Studies*, Vol. 13, No. 1, pp. 1-25.

Smith, Robert J. and Ella Lury Wiswell
    1982   *Women of Suye Mura*. Chicago: University of Chicago Press.

Smith, Thomas C.
    1955   *Political Change and Industrial Development in Japan: Government Enterprise, 1868-1880*. Stanford: Stanford University Press.
    1959   *The Agrarian Origins of Modern Japan*. Stanford: Stanford University Press.

Smith-Rosenberg, Carroll
    1986   "The Cross and the Pedestal: Women, Anti-Ritualism, and the Emergence of the American Bourgeoisie." In *Disorderly Conduct: Visions of Gender in Victorian America*. New York: Oxford University Press.

Sponberg, Alan and Helen Hardacre, editors
    1988   *Maitreya, the Future Buddha*. Cambridge: Cambridge University Press.

Sugano, Kimiko
    1982   *Kimiko's World*. San Francisco: Strawberry Hill Press.

Taira, Koji
    1970   *Economic Development and the Labor Market in Japan*. New York: Columbia University Press.

Thompson, E.P.
  1971   "The Moral Economy of the English Crowd in the 18th
          Century," *Past and Present*, Vol. 50, pp. 76-136.

Thomsen, Harry
  1963   *The New Religions of Japan*. Rutland, VT: Charles E.
          Tuttle.

Thrupp, Sylvia L., editor
  1962   *Millennial Dreams in Action: Essays in Comparative
          Study*. New York: Humanities Press.

Tsurumi, E. Patricia
  1990   *Factory Girls: Women in the Thread Mills of Meiji
          Japan*. Princeton: Princeton University Press.

Turner, Victor
  1968   *The Drums of Affliction*. Oxford: Clarendon Press.
  1973   "The Center Out There: The Pilgrim's Goal." *History
          of Religions*, Vol. 12, pp. 191-230.
  1977   "Process, System, and Symbol: A New Anthropological
          Synthesis." *Daedalus: Discoveries and
          Interpretations -- Studies in Contemporary Scholarship*,
          Vol. I (summer), pp. 61-80.

Ushioda, Sharlie C.
  1984   "Fukuda Hideko and the Woman's World of Meiji
          Japan." In *Japan in Transition: Thought and Action in
          the Meiji Era, 1868-1912*, Hilary Conroy, Sandra T.W.
          Davis, and Wayne Patterson, eds. London and
          Toronto: Associated University Press.

Valenze, Deborah
  1985   *Prophetic Sons and Daughters: Female Preaching and
          Popular Religion in Industrial England*. Princeton:
          Princeton University Press.

Wakita, Haruko
    1984   "Marriage and Property in Premodern Japan from the Perspective of Women's History." *Journal of Japanese Studies*, Vol. 10, No. 1, pp. 73-100.

Wallace, Anthony F.C.
    1969   *The Death and Rebirth of the Seneca*. New York: Vintage Books.

Walthall, Anne
    1990   "The Family Ideology of Rural Entrepreneurs in Nineteenth Century Japan." *Journal of Social History*, Vol. 23, No. 3, pp. 463-484.
    1991   "The Life Cycle of Farm Women in Tokugawa Japan." In *Recreating Japanese Women, 1600-1945*, Gail Lee Bernstein, ed. Berkeley: University of California Press.

Weber, Max
    1963   *The Sociology of Religion*. Boston: Beacon Press (1922).

Worsley, Peter
    1968   *The Trumpet Shall Sound*. New York: Schocken Books.

Yasumaru, Yoshio
    1977   *Deguchi Nao*. Tokyo: Asahi Shimbunsha.

Young, Richard Fox
    1988   "From *Gokyō-dōgen* to *Bankyō-dōkon*: a Study in the Self-Universalization of Ōmoto." *Japanese Journal of Religious Studies*, Vol. 15, No. 4, pp. 263-286.

Yoshida, Teigo
    1967   "Mystical Retribution, Spirit Possession, and Social Structure in a Japanese Village." *Ethnology*, Vol. 6, pp. 237-262.

CORNELL EAST ASIA SERIES

For ordering information, please contact:

> *Cornell East Asia Series*
> East Asia Program
> Cornell University
> 140 Uris Hall
> Ithaca, NY 14853-7601
> USA
> (607) 255-6222.